BARRON'S BOOK NOTES

EDITH WHARTON'S

Ethan Frome

BARRON'S BOOK NOTES

EDITH WHARTON'S

Ethan Frome

BY

George Ehrenhaft
Chairman, English Department
Mamaroneck (N.Y.) High School

SERIES COORDINATOR

Murray Bromberg
Principal, Wang High School of Queens
Holliswood, New York

BARRON'S EDUCATIONAL SERIES, INC.
Woodbury, New York • London • Toronto • Sydney

ACKNOWLEDGMENTS

Our thanks to Milton Katz and Julius Liebb for their contribution to the Book Notes series.

All inquiries should be addressed to:
Barron's Educational Series, Inc.
113 Crossways Park Drive
Woodbury, New York 11797

Library of Congress Catalog Card No. 85-1337

International Standard Book No. 0-8120-3513-5

Library of Congress Cataloging in Publication Data

Ehrenhaft, George.
  Edith Wharton's Ethan Frome.

  (Barron's book notes)
  Bibliography: p. 108
  Summary: A guide to reading "Ethan Frome" with a
critical and appreciative mind. Includes background on
the author's life and times, sample tests, term paper
suggestions, and a reading list.
    1. Wharton, Edith, 1862–1937. Ethan Frome.
  [1. Wharton, Edith, 1862–1937. Ethan Frome.
  2. American literature—History and criticism] I. Title.
  II. Series.
PR3545.H16E732 1985   813'.52   85-1337
ISBN 0-8120-3513-5 (pbk.)

PRINTED IN THE UNITED STATES OF AMERICA

567   550   987654321

CONTENTS

ADVISORY BOARD

HOW TO USE THIS BOOK

You have to know how to approach literature in order to get the most out of it. This *Barron's Book Notes* volume follows a plan based on methods used by some of the best students to read a work of literature.

Begin with the guide's section on the author's life and times. As you read, try to form a clear picture of the author's personality, circumstances, and motives for writing the work. This background usually will make it easier for you to hear the author's tone of voice, and follow where the author is heading.

Then go over the rest of the introductory material—such sections as those on the plot, characters, setting, themes, and style of the work. Underline, or write down in your notebook, particular things to watch for, such as contrasts between characters and repeated literary devices. At this point, you may want to develop a system of symbols to use in marking your text as you read. (Of course, you should only mark up a book you own, not one that belongs to another person or a school.) Perhaps you will want to use a different letter for each character's name, a different number for each major theme of the book, a different color for each important symbol or literary device. Be prepared to mark up the pages of your book as you read. Put your marks in the margins so you can find them again easily.

Now comes the moment you've been waiting for—the time to start reading the work of literature. You may want to put aside your *Barron's Book Notes* volume until you've read the work all the way through. Or you may want to alternate, reading the *Book Notes* analysis of each section as soon as you have finished reading the corresponding part of the original. Before you move on, reread crucial passages you don't fully understand. (Don't take this guide's analysis for granted—make up your own mind as to what the work means.)

Once you've finished the whole work of literature, you may want to review it right away, so you can firm up your ideas about what it means. You may want to leaf through the book concentrating on passages you marked in reference to one character or one theme. This is also a good time to reread the *Book Notes* introductory material, which pulls together insights on specific topics.

When it comes time to prepare for a test or to write a paper, you'll already have formed ideas about the work. You'll be able to go back through it, refreshing your memory as to the author's exact words and perspective, so that you can support your opinions with evidence drawn straight from the work. Patterns will emerge, and ideas will fall into place; your essay question or term paper will almost write itself. Give yourself a dry run with one of the sample tests in the guide. These tests present both multiple-choice and essay questions. An accompanying section gives answers to the multiple-choice questions as well as suggestions for writing the essays. If you have to select a term paper topic, you may choose one from the list of suggestions in this book. This guide also provides you with a reading list, to help you when you start research for a term paper, and a selection of provocative comments by critics, to spark your thinking before you write.

THE AUTHOR
AND HER TIMES

It's hard to imagine a less likely author for *Ethan Frome* than Edith Wharton, for this story of a poverty-stricken, lonely farmer was written by a wealthy, middle-aged member of New York City's high society.

Edith Wharton probably never spent a day of her life inside the sort of poor New England farmhouse occupied by Ethan, his wife Zeena, and their boarder Mattie Silver. It's a world she visited only in her imagination. Even so, she draws a realistic picture of the dark, cramped, cheerless rooms of the Fromes' living quarters. And her portrayal of poor farm people has the ring of truth.

Soon after *Ethan Frome* was published, a friend of Wharton's reported that she and the author had once driven around the Berkshire hills. They had paused briefly near a run-down farm. Wharton looked at the battered, unpainted house and littered yard and said she intended to write a story about a place like that. Moreover, Wharton claimed to have spent "an hour" at a Lenox, Massachusetts meetinghouse observing the speech and manner of the local citizens, and trying to imagine what their lives must be like. But whether Edith Wharton ever spoke with them, shared a meal with them, or visited them in their homes is not known. It's not very probable because the social gap was just too wide.

Wharton was accustomed to life on New York's

fashionable Fifth Avenue. At least that's where she was born Edith Jones on January 24, 1862. To avoid the turmoil of the Civil War, her parents—George and Lucretia Jones—took their family to Europe, where life was safer. Before she was ten, Wharton had lived in Rome and Paris. She had toured Spain and Germany and wintered on the French Riviera.

The Jones family returned to New York in 1872 and settled into their East Side brownstone. Instead of going to school, Wharton had tutors. Instead of a circle of friends her own age, Wharton had her family. And instead of the usual toys and amusements of most children, Wharton had her father's ample library, where she read hungrily.

In the 1870s girls of Wharton's social class generally did what their parents told them to do. What filled her parents' lives filled Edith's too: Parisian fashions, planning dinner parties and balls, the problems with maids and butlers, where to spend the holidays—the rituals of a plush red-velvet life.

One thing that set Wharton apart from other society girls was her love of writing. She made up stories and wrote poetry. Offered the choice of an evening with books and writing paper or going to a party, Wharton would probably have stayed home. She felt shy and uncomfortable with strangers and grew bored with dinner-table and drawing-room conversation. Books and learning delighted her more than the social whirl.

Soon after her society debut Wharton's father fell ill. Hoping to regain his health in a milder climate, he took the family to southern Europe. Wharton's time on the continent opened her eyes to the world. She met cultured Europeans who talked about art, books, and ideas. With them,

Wharton felt at home and soon built a reputation as an intelligent and witty young woman.

At twenty-three Wharton met and married Edward "Teddy" Wharton, a friend of her brother. It's hard to imagine a more mismatched couple. He loved the out-of-doors and the life of a sportsman, while she cared for books, European culture, and scholarship. Do opposites attract? Perhaps they do, but in this case the attraction wore off quickly. The marriage was a failure, but divorce was out of the question—too scandalous for people of the Whartons' stature. Instead, Edith and Teddy lived in misery for the better part of thirty years. At last in 1913, Edith overcame her sense of duty to her husband. She cast aside fears of being considered a "divorced woman," and ended her marriage.

Except for a few fanciful romances, Wharton's early works spring chiefly from her experience and thought. Many readers have also noted the influence of the American writer Henry James (1843-1916) on both the form and content of Wharton's works. Some of Wharton's writing is set in Europe, where she and Teddy lived for months each year. They concern the artist's place in society and contrast European and American culture. Others are tales of cheating husbands, marital conflict, and, in *The House of Mirth* (1905), an ambitious woman's struggle to achieve wealth and position in New York society. With *The House of Mirth* Wharton became a celebrity. Within two months of publication the novel broke sales records, and Wharton was assured of a permanent place among the best American authors.

In spite of general discord, Wharton and her husband enjoyed a few periods of harmony. In

1901 they decided to design and build a wonderful country house in Lenox, Massachusetts. They called it "The Mount," and lived in the house on and off for several years. Wharton portrayed the Lenox area when she wrote *Ethan Frome*, published in 1911. Starkfield, the small farming village in the novel, is much like any of numerous little towns that dot the New England countryside. Although much of Ethan's story takes place in winter, the Whartons never spent a winter at The Mount. Wharton never knew firsthand the harrowing cold and bleak landscape, which weigh so heavily on Ethan and the other characters.

But Wharton knew much too well the frustration of a failed marriage—such as Ethan and Zeena's. Teddy Wharton was thirteen years older than his wife and a totally unsuitable mate for her. She bored him, and he scoffed at her literary and intellectual pursuits. Meanwhile, she found Teddy shallow, about as exciting as a kitchen stool.

When Teddy's health began to fail, the marriage became still more strained. He crabbed and complained much of the time. In fits of temper he verbally abused his wife. Twice he suffered nervous breakdowns. For the record Edith Wharton told the story of her marriage in various writings, including her literary autobiography, *A Backward Glance* (1934). Since Teddy didn't write, we don't know his side of the story. If Edith's version is accurate, though, she wins our sympathy as the wronged partner in the marriage, just as most readers sympathize with Ethan Frome for being stuck with Zeena, his sickly, ill-tempered wife. But Ethan's is also a one-sided story. We can only guess what Zeena thinks about him by reading between the lines.

It seems certain, however, that *Ethan Frome* is a product of Edith Wharton's long and serious contemplation of the mutual obligations of marriage partners. Ethan chose to die rather than stay with his spouse. That wasn't a satisfactory solution for Wharton, though. In 1913, two years after *Ethan Frome* was published, she filed for divorce.

Ethan Frome surprised Edith Wharton's fans because it differed from all her previous books. Its heartbreaking story gripped the reading public, and the book became very popular. However, some critics didn't like it. Many thought that Wharton shouldn't have strayed from her themes of New York society. Ethan, they claimed, was not a New Englander, and Starkfield was not the New England they knew. Snow in New England is not somber; it is vibrant and bright and makes your cheeks rosy. They felt that the forlorn landscape of the novel belonged somewhere else.

Nevertheless, Ethan's powerful tragedy has attracted readers from that day to the present. The book continues to be widely read and reread. It also marked a crossroads in Edith Wharton's writing career, for she discovered that she could write books which were different from the novels of manners that had made her famous.

In *The Custom of the Country* (1913) Wharton took her readers to the Midwest, to New York, and to France, intending to poke fun at wealthy but coarse people. Perhaps she had her ex-husband in mind. She spent most of the World War I years in Paris, giving generously of her time and money to care for French children displaced by the war. Out of this experience came a book describing her relief work, *Fighting France, From Dunkerque to Belfort* (1915), and two novels, *The Marne* (1918) and *A Son at the Front* (1923).

Edith Wharton remained abroad after the war and rarely stopped writing. She completed dozens of additional novels before her death in 1937 in France. One of them, *The Age of Innocence*, has achieved the status of an American classic. Published in 1920, the book won the Pulitzer Prize. Here Wharton returned to the world she knew best, the loftiest circle of New York society in the 1870s. Rather than presenting life in old New York sentimentally, however, she points out its faults. Despite its setting, *The Age of Innocence* is not an old-fashioned novel. People continue to read it. Like *Ethan Frome* it contains a story that Edith Wharton prepared to write during much of her life.

Critics generally agree that the novels Wharton wrote during the last part of her career fall short of excellence. Perhaps she couldn't adapt her craft to the modern American scene. At the same time, however, she produced some first-rate short stories. A collection of Edith Wharton's complete works fills several library shelves. While browsing among those books, you'll surely find some of the best American literature of the twentieth century.

THE NOVEL

The Plot

If you've ever been lonely, even when surrounded by others, you know just how Ethan Frome felt most of his life. An intense, painful loneliness does things to you: You lose confidence; you feel sorry for yourself; you blame others for your pain. And sometimes, if you hurt as much as Ethan, you consider doing away with yourself.

Most of Ethan's story takes place during a winter many years ago in a small farm community in New England. In those days it was easy to be lonely. Long workdays left little time for fun. Cold and snow kept you from seeing your neighbors and friends for long stretches of time.

When you first meet Ethan, he's fifty-two years old. From his looks, though, you'd think he was much older. His shoulders sag, he limps, and his face is grim. Every day he comes to town, checks the post office for mail (he rarely has any), says barely a word to anyone, and drives off again.

Ethan's odd looks and behavior arouse the curiosity of a young stranger, in town to do an engineering job for the local power company. By chance, during a terrible blizzard the man finds overnight refuge in Ethan's house. Later, he tells you what he has discovered about Ethan.

Ethan, at eighteen, is a bright, eager scholar. He goes to college to study physics and natural science, but he drops out after a year because his father is killed in an accident. At that point Ethan loses whatever chances he has to escape the quiet and solitary life of a poor farmer. The family farm and sawmill become his responsibilities.

In spite of very hard work year after year, he earns barely enough to support himself and his mother. As his mother's health worsens, he neglects the farm and mill to care for her. But finally help arrives. Zeena Pierce, a cousin from the next valley, comes to nurse the old woman during her last illness. Fearing loneliness after his mother's death, Ethan asks Zeena to marry him, which she does.

But within a year Ethan knows that he has made a mistake. Zeena becomes chronically ill. As a semi-invalid, she does little more than nag and complain. Despite his return to misery, Ethan does his duty. He struggles to keep the farm and mill going. What money he earns goes to pay for Zeena's doctors and for medicines that never seem to work.

After six depressing years something happens to change Ethan's life forever. Mattie Silver, a distant cousin of Zeena's, moves in to help Zeena with the household chores. To Ethan, Mattie is a breath of spring—cheerful, kind, and pretty. Also, she admires Ethan's knowledge of nature. He falls for her immediately.

Zeena, however, fails to appreciate Mattie's qualities. In fact, Mattie just doesn't meet Zeena's expectations as a housekeeper. When Zeena threatens to dismiss her, you can imagine how Ethan objects. However, he can't speak up for Mattie too forcefully because he can't let Zeena know how attached he has become to the girl. His greatest worry is that she already knows.

Although Ethan wants to tell Mattie his feelings, he can't because he's tongue-tied. Adding to his misery, he's jealous of every young man who smiles at Mattie or dances with her at a church social. Meanwhile, Mattie conceals her feelings toward him. Since neither knows what the other feels, Ethan, at least, agonizes in uncertainty.

About a year after Mattie's arrival, Zeena goes overnight to Bettsbridge to visit a cousin and to consult a new doctor. Ethan is thrilled to be rid of her, even for twenty-four hours. One thing bothers him, however. On her trip Zeena is sure to spend too much money on medical treatment. Not for the first time he wishes Zeena would die.

That evening at home, alone with Mattie for once, Ethan enjoys the illusion of being married to her. But the beauty of the evening is marred by a slight accident. Zeena's cat knocks her mistress' favorite and most valued glass pickle-dish off the dinner table. Mattie is horrified because she knows that Zeena never used the dish, not even for important occasions. Although Ethan assures Mattie that he will glue the dish together the next day, Zeena returns before he can do it. When she finds the dish in pieces, she berates Ethan and insults Mattie.

Zeena brings bad news from the doctor. Her condition is so grave that she must do absolutely no work in the house. Therefore, she announces, she's hired a new girl who will arrive tomorrow evening.

Ethan explodes. Angry words spew from his lips. He thinks Zeena's sickness is part of a scheme to keep him in poverty and to force Mattie out of the house. He almost hits Zeena, but holds back at the last instant.

Mattie must leave. Of that there is no doubt because once Zeena has made up her mind, that's it! Mattie, however, has no place to go. The best she can do is return alone to her hometown and hope to find some type of work.

Late that night Ethan makes a decision. He's going to run away with Mattie the next day. He'll take her to the West, find work, divorce Zeena, and start all over again. He starts to write a good-bye letter to Zeena but stops cold when he realizes that he doesn't have the money to go West.

One last hope to raise money occurs to him. Mr. Hale, a builder in town, owes him for a lumber delivery. The bill is due in three months, but Ethan will lie to Hale. He'll say that Zeena's illness necessitates immediate payment. Then, with the money in his pocket, he and Mattie will escape to the West.

On his way to collect, Ethan meets Mrs. Hale, the builder's wife. She knows about Zeena's latest illness and praises Ethan for standing by Zeena through all her years of sickness. "You've had an awful mean time, Ethan Frome," she says.

No one has ever spoken to Ethan like this. No one has ever understood his plight like Mrs. Hale. He's suddenly overcome with guilt to think that he was about to deceive Hale. Ethan turns toward home, resigned to remain on his farm.

Now comes the most dreaded time of his life—bidding Mattie good-bye. Driving to the station, Ethan and Mattie recall the good times they've shared during the past year. Unable to contain themselves any longer, each confesses love for the other. They despair to think of never being together again. To delay their moment of parting, they decide—just for fun—to coast down the town's most perilous hill on a sled. Down, down they go, with Ethan steering skillfully past the big elm tree at a bend in the course.

At the top again, Mattie turns and cries, "Ethan, take me down again . . . so 't we'll never come up any more." At first Ethan thinks Mattie is crazy, but the thought of going home to his hateful wife persuades him he'd rather die with Mattie than live with Zeena. They mount the sled and kiss for the last time. The sled dives down the hill and crashes head-on into the massive trunk of the elm tree. But somehow they both survive.

That concludes the narrator's account of Ethan's past. Abruptly the story returns to that snowy night in Ethan's house. A tall gray-haired woman serves an unappetizing dinner. It's Zeena, as grim as ever. Sitting hunched over by the stove is a small, help-less woman, crippled for life with a spinal injury. She, of course, is Mattie. More precisely, she is what Mattie has become during the twenty-four years since the smash-up.

The night of the smash-up Zeena rose from her sickbed and never went back. All this time she has dutifully cared for Mattie. It's said that Zeena and Mattie bark at each other constantly. During their fights the one who suffers most is Ethan. Is it any wonder he looks old and worn-out?

Back in town the narrator's landlady has the last word on Ethan and his life's burdens. Maybe it would have been better if Mattie had died in the crash, she says. At least then Ethan could have lived. Now there's little difference between being a Frome on the farm and a Frome in the grave.

The Characters

Ethan Frome

If Ethan Frome could relive his life, what do you think he would be? He was miserable as a farmer, so he certainly wouldn't pick that life again. But he might not be suited for anything else.

Doctor? He had plenty of medical experience caring for family members. He wasn't much good at it, though, because he needed to summon help during his mother's last illness. He didn't like the work, either, because it confined him. When Zeena was sick he felt trapped. Once Mattie became an invalid, Ethan left the house as much as he could. Why else did he check an empty mailbox at the Starkfield post office every day? He never talked to anyone there. Of course, his daily trips to town might have been his way of keeping in touch with the outside world.

Businessman? Not on your life. Think how easily Mr. Hale weasels out of paying his debt to Ethan. Besides, a man of commerce needs self-confidence. Ethan wavers over the slightest decisions and constantly changes his mind. Recall how Ethan hides in the shadows outside the church, too ill-at-ease to step forward and take Mattie's arm. Moreover, to succeed in business, you need vision, but you can't be a visionary like Ethan. Sometimes he mistakes illusion for reality and vice-versa. For example, in his fantasy world he travels to the West with Mattie. In reality, he doesn't have the money to go.

If Ethan tried to be a salesman, he'd be no better off. People would scatter. He's too stiff and grizzled and looks as though he were "dead and in hell." Even as a young man he had a hard time with people. In college they called him "Old Stiff," and he kept largely to himself.

That's why he might fail as a lawyer, too. In fact, he'd probably be unsuited to any job which required him to speak articulately more than a sentence at a time. Words defeated him. He could never think of the right thing to say. Even when he did—because he had a good mind—the words got stuck. He couldn't even tell Mattie that he loved her. That was a shame, too, because if she had known sooner, they might have run off and lived happily ever after.

At times words cause Ethan another kind of problem. He blurts things out that he'd like to retract the instant the words pass his lips. For example, he lies to Zeena about why she must go to the train without him. Because of his lie, he realizes too late that he will need to ask Hale for money. He knows, too, that Hale won't pay. Meanwhile Zeena, believing Ethan has money, will spend far more in Bettsbridge than he can afford. Such impulsiveness would keep Ethan from succeeding at any job that required quick thinking and careful use of words.

What, then, could Ethan qualify for? He could do any manual work very well. He has a strong back, broad shoulders, and the drive to work long hours. For years he's proved himself as a persevering farmer and sawmill operator. Unfortunately, however, Starkfield is an economically depressed place. No matter how hard Ethan works, he's never more than a few steps from the poorhouse.

While Ethan may lack the personality to succeed at many jobs, he is intelligent, and he's well informed about the ways of nature. He studied science in college for a year and probably would have succeeded as an engineer or physicist had he not been summoned home to run the family farm and mill. After that he allowed himself to be trapped. His mother's illness, his marriage to Zeena, his poverty—even the isolated town of Starkfield—eroded his will to break away. Soon he stopped trying.

Nevertheless, Ethan continued to search for "huge cloudy meanings behind the daily face of things." Despite his troubled life, he's still one of the "smart ones," according to his fellow townsman, Harmon Gow. In other words, Ethan is a thinker, a philosopher.

To which school of philosophy does he belong? Surely it must be that which silently accepts the world as it is. That is, Ethan is a stoic. He knows he can't change his lot in life, although he once thought to escape from it. When he failed, he became silently resigned to it. Ultimately, that may be the real tragedy of Ethan Frome.

Mattie Silver

Scan almost any passage that alludes to Mattie and you will find images galore that reveal her sweet, pure, and lively youthfulness. She may be too good to be true. Since you see Mattie through Ethan's eyes, she can do no wrong. But is she really as flawless as Ethan believes? Strip off the rose-colored glasses and look.

Mattie can't make the grade as a housekeeper. Ethan, who is busy enough all day, needs to help her complete her chores. In fact, she has failed at every job she's held. Back in Stamford, her home-town, she tried stenography, bookkeeping, and store-clerking, all without success. When Zeena sends her away, Ethan fears that she'll end up walking the streets.

Passing Shadow Pond during their ride to the train, Mattie is surprised to learn that Ethan has loved her for months. But more shocking is that she didn't know before. Is she that insensitive? For a year Ethan has run to her side at every chance. He has helped her, looked starry-eyed at her, and hung on her every word and gesture. And she hasn't noticed?

Mattie confesses her love for Ethan. Is she say-ing the truth? If so, why has she regularly gone to church dances without him and flirted with Denis Eady, too?

The pickle-dish broke because Mattie, despite knowing its value to Zeena, removed it from the closet. Why? To please a man married to someone else. How much merit is there in Zeena's charge, then, that Mattie is sneaky? It's a question for you to ponder.

None of these shortcomings matters to Ethan, of course, because he's blinded by love. When Mattie compares a sunset to a painting—as though nature mimicked art—Ethan is charmed. Someone of another mind would call Mattie just a foolish girl.

Compared to Zeena, of course, Mattie is a saint. She's pretty, sweet-tempered, and affectionate. Although Zeena's abuse hurts her, she always bounces back as perky as ever. When Zeena scolds, Mattie listens without fighting back. When pain keeps Zeena from sleep, Mattie says, "I'm so sorry, Zeena! Isn't there anything I can do?"

Mattie gives Ethan new life. For the first time in his twenty-eight years he has a soul mate. They walk together, sharing the beauties of nature. She's fascinated by his lectures on the stars and on rock formations. Like a schoolgirl, she admires his knowledge with wide-eyed wonder. At the same time, she has the ability, with a word or a look, to send Ethan into a dark mood or somber state of mind.

Almost every place Mattie appears in the book, images of light and warmth accompany her. Words such as *fire, star, glow, shining*—a thesaurus of synonyms—indicate why Mattie's last name is *Silver*. She brightens Ethan's life and stands out luminously against the dark, cold setting of the story. You'll also find the color red in Mattie's lips, cheeks, and clothes. Why red? For one, it's the color of love. It also sets Mattie apart from the blacks, whites, and grays used to depict almost everything else in the book.

Although she has a right to be downhearted, Mattie shows no aftereffects of the trials she's endured. Just prior to settling in Starkfield she lost her mother and father. Her family turned their backs on her because her late father—not she—owed them money. At twenty-one she was an outcast with no home, no job, and no prospects. Her only bit of luck was that Zeena, her distant cousin, needed someone to help around the house. Thus Mattie moved in with the Fromes.

When Mattie arrives, Ethan is ready for love. After seven years of marriage to Zeena, he can hardly help falling for Mattie. And Mattie, after tasting loneliness, needs someone, too. Each fills a void in the other's life. But just a year later, Mattie's dismissal threatens to cast them into isolation again.

During their final moments together Mattie proposes suicide to Ethan. Is her love for him so intense that she can't live without him? Or does the thought of loneliness terrorize her so much that she'd rather die? Perhaps her desperation derives both from love and fear. Regardless, the result is shocking.

It's hard to imagine a more tragic ending. Mattie could have died in the sled smash-up. Unfortunately, fate cannot be outwitted so easily. Mattie, who dreaded being alone, must live as a cripple, forever dependent on others. Pain transforms her into an old crone long before her time. Instead of love, she offers Ethan woe. What cruel ironies!

Perhaps it's tempting to draw a moral from Mattie's tale—something about the perils of meddling in the life of a married man. But Edith Wharton probably had no such moral in mind. She intended not to preach proper behavior, but to explore the tragic possibilities of life.

Zenobia (Zeena) Frome

Don't be surprised if you cringe while reading about Zeena Frome. Edith Wharton took pains to make her one of the most unappealing people imaginable—the sort who creates a chill wherever she goes. You may know someone like her. You can count on your fingers the number of times she smiles in a month. She rarely opens her mouth except to criticize and complain. But she doesn't need words to tell you what she thinks, for she wears a face of perpetual disapproval.

As you read the novel, be alert to some of Zeena's

redeeming qualities, and try to be a little sympathetic. She's too important a character to be one-dimensional. Remember that *Ethan Frome* is a story envisioned by a narrator who is not altogether impartial. Although you may also side with Ethan, you shouldn't turn totally against Zeena. Think, for example, of how she has cared for Mattie during the twenty-four years before you meet Ethan on the steps of the Starkfield post office.

By that time, of course, Ethan has endured more than thirty years of misery as Zeena's husband. He blames Zeena for ruining his life. Ever since their wedding, she has held him captive. One of the reasons he married her was because he owed her a debt of gratitude after she had cared for his mother on her deathbed. Can you expect a marriage born of one partner's obligation to the other to succeed?

As Ethan's new wife, Zeena refused to move to the city, although earlier she had agreed to do so. As a result, Ethan was forced to stay on the farm and do his best to make a living there. Then Zeena developed a chronic illness that permanently ended Ethan's hope for escape. Almost every penny he earned went toward paying for doctors and useless patent medicines. Finally, she grew silent. She hardly left the house and talked to no one, except to nag and complain. In effect, she severed her ties with life.

You will probably notice that almost every time you find a reference to cold, darkness, sickness, or death in the story, Zeena, or an allusion to her, will appear. She walks through the book like a plague, spreading gloom on nearly every page. When you first see her—at the kitchen door—she's the picture of ugliness. The kitchen itself "had the deadly chill of a vault." Obviously, the storyteller is stacking the cards against Zeena for a purpose.

As a cold, isolated, and grim figure, Zeena embodies her surroundings. You can hardly separate her from the wintry Starkfield landscape. Like the town, tucked by itself in a lonesome valley, Zeena has removed herself from society. She is consumed by her illness, which she uses to control Ethan. By being a semi-invalid, she can tell Ethan what to do. She can also use her condition to justify anything she cares to do. Even so, Ethan doubts the authenticity of some of his wife's ailments. For example, he would argue that Zeena went to Bettsbridge not to see a new doctor but to spend money.

You might wonder why Ethan doesn't simply walk out on Zeena. Many modern hubands would, but in Ethan's day most husbands and wives held to their marriage vows until death. Still, nothing in Ethan and Zeena's relationship is worth preserving. He despises her. She's repugnant to him in so many ways—from her false teeth to her asthmatic breathing. Worst of all, she has the knack of making Ethan feel guilty about almost everything he does and thinks, especially after Mattie Silver arrives on the farm. A certain look on Zeena's face or an offhand comment gives Ethan the eerie feeling that she knows what he's thinking. She haunts him. Even when he and Mattie are hurtling down the hill on their fateful sled ride, Zeena appears in his mind's eye. He is stuck with her, no matter what. Ethan's bungled attempt to escape with Mattie attests to that.

Although she's easy to scorn, Zeena may also deserve a little understanding. Most of her life she has cared for sick people, first Ethan's mother and then Mattie. When she ran out of others to care for, she tended to herself. True, she may have brought on her own illnesses, but self-imposed ailments cause just as much suffering as other diseases. Also, she bears the burdens of an unsightly face, and for a year at least, a husband who would be unfaithful if he had the courage. Think, too, of how pathetic she seems during the incident of the broken pickle-dish. She weeps over a broken glass dish, her most valued possession. How petty, yes, but can't you sympathize with someone whose life has been such a waste?

In the end, of course, Zeena comes through. She rises from her sickbed, never to return. For twenty-four years she cares for Mattie, the woman who tried to steal her husband. Does she redeem herself by responding so unselfishly to Mattie's tragedy? Can she be forgiven, after all, for all the misery she has spread? While you may not like Zeena any more than you did earlier, can you at least admire her charity?

Narrator

The nameless narrator appears in the prologue and in the epilogue of the novel. He's a young engineer with time to kill in Starkfield. Ethan Frome's odd appearance arouses his curiosity. With the instinct of a detective, he asks the town residents about Ethan, and with the skill of an accomplished writer he constructs Ethan's story from the bits and pieces of information he has collected.

Denis Eady

Denis is a cheerful young man in Starkfield whom Ethan despises mainly because he is an eligible bachelor. Ethan perceives Denis as an archrival for Mattie's affection. Years later Denis becomes the town's "rich Irish grocer."

Jotham Powell

Jotham, Ethan's hired hand, helps take care of the farm and mill. He doesn't say much, but he knows trouble when he sees it. He slips quietly out of sight when Zeena and Ethan are about to have the argument of their lives over Mattie's future.

Mr. Andrew Hale

Mr. Hale buys lumber from Ethan for building houses. Unfortunately, he doesn't pay on delivery but waits three months. Ethan, therefore, lacks the money to escape with Mattie from Zeena. Mr. Hale is also the father of Ned, who marries Ruth Varnum.

Mrs. Andrew Hale

Mrs. Hale is probably the friendliest person in Starkfield. Her kindness so startles Ethan that he abandons his plan to collect money from Mr. Hale. Ethan's conscience won't permit him to deceive the husband of someone as understanding as Mrs. Hale.

Mrs. Ruth Varnum Hale

Ruth is the landlady of the Varnum house, where the novel's narrator stays during his time in Starkfield. She was the first to see Ethan and Mattie after the sled smash-up. Somewhat more refined than other Starkfielders, she recognizes the miserable life Ethan has led since his encounter with the elm tree.

Harmon Gow

Starkfield's stage driver, Harmon tells the narrator a little bit about Ethan. He knows what too many winters in Starkfield can do to a man.

Other Elements

SETTING

In the summertime the hills of New England now swarm with tourists. In winter they're alive with skiers. But it hasn't always been that way. In Ethan Frome's time, around the turn of the century, the countryside is a cold and lifeless place. In fact, Edith Wharton takes pains to show you how desolate it is.

She calls Ethan's small farming community *Stark*field, and the town lives up to its name. It's desolate and its people are poor. Some, like Ethan, can barely scrape a living off the rocky, barren land.

Life is dreary and cheerless in Starkfield. Only an occasional church social breaks the monotony. For months every year snow lies heavily on the hills, fields, and villages. People stay indoors and keep to themselves. Weeks pass between visits with friends or neighbors. Surely no place in Massachusetts can really be as grim as Starkfield.

Why did Edith Wharton invent such a site for her novel? You might find an answer in the character of Ethan Frome himself. Doesn't the countryside often mirror his own emotional landscape? That is, when Ethan feels despair the land and sky grow dark and oppressive. When Ethan's mood lightens, there's considerable beauty all around. Ethan spends his happiest hours with Mattie roaming the lovely woodlands and walking under the stars.

Because Ethan is melancholy more often than he's merry, Starkfield seems like a sad and dismal place. To be sure, there's life in the village proper, but leave the main street and you find only battered little houses strewn here and there among the hills.

Starkfield afflicts Ethan and helps to shape his destiny. Like the town, he is sullen and run-down. Starkfield sits alone in its valley, isolated from the world around it. Ethan is isolated too. He left the lonely valley to go to college, but since returning he has gone scarcely more than a few miles from his remote farm. Physically, and therefore, emotionally, he is trapped by his wife, his farm, and his poverty.

Not everyone in Starkfield feels oppressed. For example, Ned Hale and Ruth Varnum relish their life and their love. What's the trouble with Ethan, then? Why can't he rise above the oppressive atmosphere? Possibly he's too sensitive. He absorbs his surroundings like a sponge. He is like a piece of the scenery, or as the narrator says, "a part of the mute melancholy landscape, an incarnation of frozen woe." And he lacks the strength to shake himself loose before it's too late.

THEMES

You'd never doubt that *Ethan Frome* is a somber book after glancing at the themes listed here. There's not a reassuring one among them. Yes, a tragic story evokes tragic themes. But among the tragic circumstances of some stories a faint ray of hope— a statement about man's nobility, perhaps—sometimes shines through. There seems to be no such beacon in *Ethan Frome*.

1. LONELINESS/ISOLATION

In college Ethan acquired the nickname "Old Stiff" because he rarely went out with the boys. Once he returned to the farm he couldn't go out with them even if he had wanted to. Whatever he's done has kept him apart from others: tending the farm and mill, nursing his sick mother, caring for Zeena.

Ventures outside the bounds of his farm have usually brought Ethan no luck. He's inept doing business with Mr. Hale. Denis Eady and his cronies make fun of him. The one time he plans to run away with Mattie, the effort fails. A few kind words spoken by Mrs. Hale shock him into realizing that he will never escape.

Ethan's isolation is intensified because he is often tongue-tied. He'd like to make contact with others but can't. For example, when he wants to dazzle Mattie with beautiful words of love, he mutters, "Come along."

In their own ways, Zeena and Mattie are solitary figures, too. For years, Zeena rarely leaves the house. She's consumed by her illness. Mattie, on the other hand, seeks refuge from loneliness at the Fromes' farm. A year later she chooses to die rather then return to a world of solitude.

2. SILENT "GRANITE OUTCROPPINGS"

Edith Wharton once wrote that with *Ethan Frome* she intended to present a story that told elemental truths about the sturdy, silent character of life in the New England hills. She wanted to reveal New England's "granite outcroppings."

You need to be tough—like granite—to endure winters like those described in the novel. Month after month of dreary skies, snow-covered lands, and bitter cold can erode your spirit. You must fight depression and loneliness. Above all, you must love silence. If you must turn on the radio at every quiet moment, you'd probably go mad in Ethan's world.

You hear the silence of Starkfield even when people talk. Sound issues from their mouths, but the words mean nothing. On their night of nights Ethan and Mattie engage in small talk—words to fill a vacuum, nothing more. Deep inside, Ethan speaks eloquently, but no one hears him. To the people of Starkfield, he's a silent ghost-like figure who prefers to mind his own business.

3. HOPELESSNESS

The proverb about trying again when at first you don't succeed sounds good, but it's hard to live by. What discourages people more than repeated failure?

Ethan is an expert on failure. In his youth he had hoped to study science, but family sickness and death dashed his hopes. After he married Zeena, he intended to sell the farm and move to the city, but his bride put an end to that dream.

For years all his time and energy have been put into the farm and mill. Yet the monotonous work gives him little satisfaction. What money he earns Zeena uses to buy medicines. He can't escape with Mattie because he can't afford the fare. His one big effort to break out of his prison—that is, to destroy his life—ends in disaster. After the smash-up he's locked forever in a living hell. As Mrs. Hale observes, there's little difference between the grave and the farm for Ethan Frome.

4. "TIL DEATH DO US PART"

Ethan and Zeena's marriage is built on a flimsy foundation. After his mother dies, Ethan asks Zeena to stay with him on the farm because the thought of living there alone terrifies him. What hope is there for such a marriage?

Ethan realizes his mistake after only a few months. But there's no remedy; he remains bound by his marriage vows. In fact, he is virtually enslaved by them.

Even when Mattie enters his life, Ethan remains true to his pledge to Zeena. He's not above wishing that Zeena would die, however. And he's more than willing to pretend, at least for an evening, that he's married to Mattie instead of Zeena.

Zeena's decision to dismiss Mattie convinces Ethan to desert his wife. But as he writes his goodbye letter his conscience shatters his dream of starting over in the West with Mattie.

How firmly Ethan is tied to Zeena! Even his attempt to take his leave by killing himself fails. After the smash-up, he is fated to be with her forever, even in the grave.

5. THE TYRANNY OF SICKNESS

When a chronic illness strikes, the patient is not the only one who suffers. Friends and family bear the pain, too. Ethan Frome's story confirms how despotic an illness can be. Because of others' infirmity, Ethan's ambitions are thwarted. He drops out of college, lets his farm and mill fall into ruin, and remains in poverty.

Ethan lives in a world dominated by sick people. His father is kicked by a horse and dies after a long illness. His mother survives as a semi-invalid for years. And Zeena is an established sick person, notable in Starkfield for her "condition."

Ethan suspects that some of Zeena's symptoms are feigned, but he has no proof. If you consider how she uses her illness to control him, you might suspect she exaggerates her pain sometimes. Whether feigned or not, Zeena's ailments keep Ethan down on the farm. The one time he almost escapes, Mrs. Hale pays him tribute for being so devoted to his sick wife. Ashamed of himself for contemplating escape, Ethan returns home, resigned to his fate.

The cruelest irony of all, Ethan's attempt to flee, concludes with a crippling smash-up. Mattie's spinal injury seals Ethan's destiny permanently.

6. DEATH'S DOMINION

Starkfield is dead, no matter how you define the word. It's dead in the sense of having no action on Saturday night—or on any other night for that matter.

Most of the story takes place in the depths of winter, when life drains from trees and plants, animals hibernate, and water stops flowing. Even the people, to escape from winter's deathlike grip, entomb themselves inside small, wooden, snow-buried houses.

Outside Ethan's door lie all his ancestors. He reads their gravestones, and the words remind him of his ties to the farm, the house, and the mill. He can't escape and he expects to lie there, too, some day.

Could you call Zeena alive? Although she moves and breathes, she has cut herself off from life. In a word, she is figuratively dead. After the smash-up, Mattie and Ethan join her in the land of the living dead.

7. ILLUSION VS. REALITY

What is illusion? What is reality? Edith Wharton's book challenges you to come to grips with these age-old questions. Can you find the equivalent of Starkfield in the real New England? Or are the town and its people merely products of Wharton's fantasy? As you get to know them better, you'll be able to make up your own mind.

No one can accuse Ethan of being a realist, for he leads a rich fantasy life. He has spells of illusion that vanish like bubbles in the air. The illusion of being married to Mattie shatters when the glass pickle-dish crashes to the floor. Repeatedly, Ethan thinks he's noticed signs of Mattie's affection for him, but more often than not her smiles and gestures mean nothing.

Does Zeena know what Ethan feels for Mattie? Sometimes she seems to, but then again, she seems not to. Ethan sifts her every word and deed, searching for clues. When Zeena discharges Mattie, Ethan can't believe it. He deludes himself into thinking that Zeena will change her mind in the morning.

At the height of his distress Ethan fancies himself running away with Mattie, divorcing Zeena, and enjoying a prosperous life in the West. Reality intrudes, however. He can't pay for one ticket West, much less two.

How appropriate it is that Mattie and Ethan first found love at a place called Shadow Pond. Like a shadow, their love is fleeting. Now you see it, now you don't.

STYLE

You won't find many novels shorter than *Ethan Frome* in a library of American classics. (It's often called a *novelette*, rather than a novel.) At the same time you won't find many so carefully crafted. Edith Wharton leaves nothing to chance. She has a reason for every bit of action and each descriptive passage. She chooses details with the greatest care—from names of places and people to the furniture in a room. If you like digging for meanings beneath the surface of a story, you've come to the right place.

To tell her story of plain country people, Wharton uses simple, direct language. At times it's almost "stark"—clipped, clear, and efficient. Her characters speak in their native dialect, and this makes sense. Who would want to read a story about country folk who talk like English teachers?

At first glance Ethan Frome passes as a plain, maybe even dull, New England farmer. Up close, however, you discover great complexity in the man. Sometimes you can hardly keep up with him. For example, one moment he's gleeful, the next he's glum. The contrasts you find in Ethan's moods appear again and again in imagery throughout the story.

Brightness is often set off against gloominess. You discover contrasts of light and dark on almost every page. Of course, you associate light with Ethan's high spirits, with Mattie (note that her last name is *Silver*), and with love. Darkness, as you might expect, suggests the opposite. When you first meet Zeena, she stands in the dark background of the kitchen.

The same contrast holds true for cold and warmth. Everything about Zeena is cold and harsh. (Note that *Pierce* was Zeena's maiden name.) Mattie, on the other hand, radiates warmth. She always has a fire going for Ethan. Several times you are shown the same scene twice—once when Ethan is dejected, another time when his spirits soar. For example, look at the description of the land while Ethan walks home, expecting to find Zeena. Then compare it to the same view as Ethan passes by on his way home to Mattie. You'll probably be struck by the contrast in word choice between the two passages.

The novel is also crowded with descriptions containing black (shadows, spruce trees, gravestones) and white (snow, clouds). A director filming *Ethan Frome* would be well advised to use black and white—as well as red. Red, suggesting passion, appears on Mattie's lips and cheeks, and in her hair ribbons. Also, the forbidden pickle-dish, which Mattie uses to charm Ethan, is made of "gay red glass."

Of all the novel's symbols, the one that's most enduring for many readers is the pickle-dish. It may stick in your mind because it's such an unusual object. But more to the point, do you see the symbolic importance of the dish? Why, for instance, does the pickle-dish have to be broken? Could it suggest the end of Ethan and Mattie's love? If not, what influence does the shattering of the dish have on Ethan's illusion that he's married to Mattie? Might it also foretell Ethan and Mattie's smash-up near the end of the book? However you choose to interpret the incident of the pickle-dish, you can be fairly sure that you'll remember it long after many other details have faded from your memory.

Another striking symbol is Zeena's cat. The cat intrudes all through Ethan and Mattie's wonderful evening together. What purpose is served by having the cat sit in her mistress' place? Why should the cat's assault on the milk-jug lead to the smashing of the pickle-dish? Notice, too, how the cat ends Ethan's effort to have a tender moment with Mattie. Zeena herself could hardly have been a greater nuisance than the cat. When she returns from Bettsbridge, Zeena feeds and strokes the cat. Why do you think Edith Wharton inserted that scene?

POINT OF VIEW

The words of the novel come to you through the narrator, a young engineer. He tells you about the winter he spent in Starkfield, Massachusetts, several years ago while working for the local power company. As a stranger he knows no more than you about the town and people. He merely relates his observations. At the post office every day he notices a tall, grizzled customer—Ethan Frome. Ethan is so curious-looking that the narrator asks some townspeople about him. But Starkfielders are tight-lipped with strangers and reveal only a few odd bits and pieces. From these scraps the narrator constructs the story.

In a snowstorm one night the narrator finds refuge in Ethan's house. There he finds "the clue to Ethan Frome," and begins to sort out the odd bits and pieces he has heard from others.

The narrator uses his own words to tell his "vision," as he calls it, of Ethan Frome's story. Most likely he has altered details, added a description or two he never heard from a townsperson, rearranged events. He says that the story was different each time someone talked to him about it, and doesn't pretend that his "vision" is what actually happened, only what might have happened.

Edith Wharton puts her own words into the pen of the young engineer. Through him she tells her "tragedy," because he is the only person capable of understanding the whole story. To the townspeople, Ethan's story is complicated and mysterious, but the narrator has the perspective to tell it simply, and to put it in its rightful place.

FORM AND STRUCTURE

Ethan Frome is a remembrance of past events. (Wharton is said to have been very impressed by the first volume of the French writer Marcel Proust's great work, *Remembrance of Things Past*.) The most recent event happened several years ago when the narrator lived for a winter in Starkfield, Massachusetts. During that time he came to know the story of Ethan Frome.

The narrator tells you how he found out about Ethan in the introductory chapter, which serves as a prologue to the main story. In the prologue you learn about present-day Starkfield and its people. You also become acquainted with the land around the village, and you hear a few random facts about Ethan. At this point you can't tell which facts are important and which are not. One detail that impresses the narrator is that Ethan is fifty-two years old, but looks far older.

At the end of the prologue the narrator finds

himself spending the night in Ethan's house. That evening he "found the clue to Ethan Frome," and in the first chapter begins to relate an account of Ethan's life between the ages of approximately eighteen and twenty-eight.

The narrator uses Chapters I to IX to tell you the story of Ethan's tragic romance with Mattie Silver, an affair that ended twenty-four years before. But throughout the tale you find additional references to events that happened even earlier. For example, in a single chapter you might see Ethan as an eighteen-year-old college student and then eavesdrop on a conversation he had last year. Next you may witness something that happened last night.

As you read, you need to stay alert for sudden shifts in time. You may think that it's easier to read a story told chronologically. No doubt it often is, but think why in this novel it may be more fitting to leap from one part of the hero's life to another. Doesn't it resemble the way in which details of Ethan's life were revealed to the narrator? The information was unfolded in bits and pieces, not as a sequential story.

Chapter IX ends with Mattie and Ethan lying injured in the snow after their smash-up. Then comes a concluding chapter, which you might call an epilogue. In the epilogue the narrator has returned to his residence in Starkfield after a night in Ethan's farmhouse. The landlady, Mrs. Hale, tells him what happened to Ethan and Mattie after the smash-up and finishes the story with a bitter comment about life in the Frome household during the last twenty-four years. At the end you realize why Ethan appears so much older than he is.

Edith Wharton called writing *Ethan Frome* the "construction" of a picture. That's an apt description if you think of the prologue and epilogue as a kind of frame for Ethan's story. By framing the story, Wharton helps you to focus on the subject. From the very beginning you know *what* Ethan has become. You read the book to find out *how*.

The Story
PROLOGUE

One thing that sets *Ethan Frome* apart from other novels is the manner in which the story is told. Edith Wharton doesn't just start at the beginning and tell you what happens. Rather, she introduces you to a narrator who knows no more about Ethan Frome than you do.

NOTE: The narrator, who remains nameless, identifies himself as a young engineer. He tells you how he uncovered Ethan's story bit by bit. He recounts what people said to him and what he observed during the months he spent in Ethan's hometown one winter long ago.

This opening chapter is a prologue to the main story. It introduces the narrator, describes the town and surrounding countryside, gives you a glimpse at some townspeople, and starts to build some of the novel's major themes. But most of all, it stirs your curiosity about Ethan Frome.

The narrator pulls you into the book as he might

draw a stranger into a conversation over coffee. He addresses you directly: "If you know Stark-field, Massachusetts, you know the post office." The post office is where he first laid eyes on Ethan. Every day at noon Ethan parked his buggy at the curb and picked up mail at the post office window. But oddly, he rarely got anything except the local newspaper and an occasional package of patent medicine addressed to his wife, Zeena Frome.

Ethan seldom talked to anybody. When someone addressed him, he answered quietly with as few words as possible before mounting his buggy and driving slowly back to his farm. What his daily visit to town meant to him was anybody's guess.

NOTE: It's no accident that Ethan's solitude impresses the narrator. Ethan appears to be a cheerless, broken man, not the sort of fellow you'd slap on the back and invite for a beer. There are many reasons why people withdraw into themselves. Sometimes it's their nature. For others, life has been too hard. Some people stay out of others' ways so they won't get hurt. Which of these applies to Ethan, the narrator intends to find out.

Ethan catches the narrator's eye because his looks are striking. Tall and powerful, Ethan must have been a gallant figure at one time. But now he hobbles when he walks, his shoulders sag, and he has a prominent red gash, the scar of an old wound, across his forehead. To the narrator, Ethan looks as though he "was dead and in hell." Yet he is only fifty-two years old.

Harmon Gow, Starkfield's former stage driver, explains the contrast between Ethan's run-down appearance and his age: It was the "smash-up," he says, an event that occurred twenty-four years ago. (A quick subtraction shows that Ethan was twenty-eight at the time.) It was a terrible smash-up, Gow recalls, and it should have killed him. But, he adds, the Fromes are tough, and Ethan will probably live to one hundred. Considering his battered looks, the narrator finds that hard to believe.

Gow also suggests that Ethan has turned into a stiff and grizzled old man because "he's been in Starkfield too many winters. Most of the smart ones get away." Gow's remark puzzles the narrator at first, but as time passes he begins to understand what Gow meant.

The narrator, it turns out, has spent a whole winter in Starkfield. An engineer for a power company, he had been sent to do a job in nearby Corbury Junction. A strike delayed the work, so he had plenty of time to get to know the area. Winter, he tells us, "shut down on Starkfield." He paints a grim picture of an almost lifeless town held in winter's deathlike grip. For close to six months the town sags under the weight of snow, its pulse sluggish, like an animal in hibernation. Living in such a place can crush a man's spirit. Clearly, Harmon Gow knew what he was talking about when he commented that "most of the smart ones get away."

NOTE: Have you noticed how appropriately Starkfield is named? It's harsh, desolate, and barren—a tough place to spend a winter. Notice how often Starkfield's landscapes are described as "lonely," "silent," or "gloomy." People's moods and emotions often swing with changes in the weather. Also, the climate of a place rubs off on people. To some extent that may help to explain not only Ethan's austere personality, but also the somber atmosphere of the town and its surrounding countryside.

You don't know why Ethan couldn't "get away" from Starkfield. The narrator is curious, though, and tries to find out. But people in Starkfield generally don't open up to strangers, so it takes a while for him to unlock the mystery of Ethan's puzzling appearance and behavior.

He tries to construct a few pieces of the puzzle by talking to Ruth Hale, a widow known as Mrs. Ned Hale, who owns the Varnum house, where the narrator stayed during his time in Starkfield. Ruth Hale gossips endlessly about the goings-on in Starkfield, but curiously, she won't talk about Ethan Frome. When pressed to reveal some information, she murmurs, "Yes, I knew them both . . . it was awful. . . ."

Mrs. Hale's reluctance to say more raises further questions in the narrator's—to say nothing of the reader's—mind: Who are "both?" What was "it?" Why was it "awful?" And especially, why did Mrs. Hale become upset when asked about Ethan?

The narrator's quest for information takes him back to Harmon Gow, whose "uncomprehending grunt" doesn't help much, either. However, Harmon adds that "it"—presumably, the smash-up— took place near the Varnum house and that Ruth was the first person to see the victims after it happened. Now, years later, she still can't bear to talk about it.

A little later, quite by accident, the narrator's life converges with Ethan's. Their encounter gives us a chance to meet Ethan close up, and finally to learn the whole story behind this unusual behavior and appearance.

First you're told how the two men made contact. The narrator works at a powerhouse in a place called the Junction, a ten-mile commute from Starkfield. Each day he takes a buggy or sleigh provided by Denis Eady, the owner of the town's livery stable. He is dropped off in Corbury Flats, three miles away, where he catches a train to the Junction. One day in midwinter, Eady's horses "fell ill of a local epidemic." Harmon Gow advises the narrator that Ethan Frome's horse was still healthy, and for a dollar Ethan might be persuaded to drive over to the Flats each morning and back again in the afternoon.

The narrator expresses wonder that Ethan needs money so badly. "Well, matters ain't gone any too well with him," replies Gow. For the last twenty years, he continues, Ethan's had problems making ends meet on his farm. Although it's always been tough for Ethan, things had gotten even worse. His father got kicked in the head by a horse, went soft in the brain, and gave away most of his money before he died. Then Ethan's mother took sick with a disease that took years to kill her. And now Zeena Frome, Ethan's wife, is sickly, too. "Sickness and trouble: that's what Ethan's had his plate full up with, ever since the very first helping," says Gow.

Every day for a week after that, Ethan carries

the narrator back and forth to Corbury Flats. Ethan doesn't say much, answering questions in monosyllables. He hardly even looks at his passenger. To the narrator, Ethan is like a piece of the "mute, melancholy" winter landscape, a piece of "frozen woe."

NOTE: Even if you read casually, you can hardly miss the numerous references to winter in the novel. Winter, traditionally, is the season when life ebbs from the earth. It's no accident, therefore, that in scene after scene you will be reminded of death. Death, especially death in winter, is one of the novel's principal themes. You'll find out why long before you finish the book.

Only twice during many trips to and from work does Ethan emerge from his shell. Once he reveals that long ago he had briefly been in Florida, but the memory of it is now "all snowed under." Another time the narrator misplaces a popular science book on bio-chemistry. Later he sees the book in Ethan's hand. Ethan says bitterly that the book contains things "that I didn't know the first word about." Further, he discloses that he used to be interested in this type of technical book. When the narrator offers the book on loan, he hesitates, then says, "Thank you—I'll take it."

NOTE: Ethan's professed interest in science surprises the narrator. Could it also explain Ethan's willingness to talk to him? Perhaps Ethan needs a soulmate, and the young engineer fills the bill.

Ethan may strike you as very odd and remote. But a sound mind resides behind that solemn mask. Remember that Harmon Gow included Ethan among "the smart ones." Of course, there are different ways to be "smart." Did Harmon mean "clever and alert?" He couldn't have meant smart in the sense of fashionable, for Ethan is anything but that.

One day the narrator is given a once-in-a-life-time chance to unseal Ethan's lips. A heavy overnight snowfall has blocked the train to the Junction. Despite the storm, Ethan shows up as usual in the morning to take the narrator to work. Since the train is stuck, Ethan offers to drive clear over to the Junction. The narrator says, "You're doing me the biggest kind of a favour."

"That's all right," replies Ethan.

On the way the two men pass by Ethan's land. The sawmill looks "exanimate" (that is, it used to be alive and thriving, but is no longer); the sheds sag under their load of snow. In the orchard, apple trees are "starved" and "writhing." The run-down farmhouse makes the landscape "lonelier."

Ethan's house looks shrunken, and in fact, it is. Its "L" is missing. For some sad reason that he doesn't explain, Ethan had to take it down.

NOTE: As the narrator explains, the "L" in a New England farmhouse is a structure usually built at right angles to the main house. It links the living quarters to the barn or woodshed. Because it's connected to the main house, it could symbolize the farmer's link to the soil. Or its importance might be that it enabled the farmer to get to his work more comfortably on icy mornings. Either way, Ethan's house is diminished, and it's described in such detail that you can't miss the narrator's point. The house reflects the diminished life of its occupants.

Can Ethan tell what his passenger thinks about the Fromes' run-down house and sawmill? It seems so, for he launches into a partial account of his family's decline. The road running past the farm was well traveled at one time, but the coming of the railroad put an end to that. Ethan's mother, who suffered terribly from rheumatism, managed to get by as long as the traffic on the road distracted her. When nobody passed by any more, the old lady didn't understand why. "It preyed on her right along till she died," Ethan says.

For the time being, that's all you learn about Ethan's past. Although it's not much, it's a start.

Before the sleigh arrives at the Junction, snow starts to fall again, obscuring the landscape and silencing Ethan. That afternoon on the return trip it begins to snow heavily. In no time the road is buried. The old horse becomes confused and strays from the path two or three times. Daylight fades and the narrator jumps from the sleigh to guide the horse. It's a struggle for both men and beast to keep going. When they are near exhaustion, Ethan spies his farm's gate. They've made it to the Fromes' place, but to go all the way to Starkfield that night is out of the question.

Quite by chance the narrator gains access into

Ethan Frome's house, a place no stranger has entered in many, many years. Approaching the door, he hears a woman's voice inside. The quality of the voice tells him that she's complaining about something. But as he enters, the droning voice suddenly grows still.

That night the narrator says, "I found the clue to Ethan Frome." When you turn the page to Chapter I, you'll begin to hear the whole melancholy story.

CHAPTER I

Suddenly you're swept back·at least a generation to the time when Ethan Frome is a young man. You see him walking rapidly through the empty streets of Starkfield. It's a clear night and as usual in the novel, it is wintertime. Places and names you already know from the opening chapter are mentioned again, but this time in a new context.

NOTE: In *Ethan Frome* Edith Wharton "frames" Ethan's story inside two chapters (the first and last) set closer to the present than the main part of the story. The two chapters serve as a frame through which the reader views the past. You must wait until the very last part of the book to learn what the narrator saw and heard in Ethan's house that snowy night.

Perhaps you'd expect the story to be told in Ethan's words. But Edith Wharton serves up a surprise; she has the narrator tell the story as he envisions it. Like a master storyteller, he relates facts, but also shapes the tale with his imagination. As you read, try to determine which events might have actually occurred and which must be the product of the narrator's inventive mind.

Ethan walks past Michael Eady's new brick store. (He must be related to Denis Eady, whose horses will someday take the narrator to work. You'll find out.) Then there's Lawyer Varnum's house. (He's the father of Ruth Varnum. You know that years from now Ruth will be Ned Hale's widow, and the narrator will be renting a room from her in this very house.)

Just outside the Varnum gates lies the road to Corbury, with its steep slope. The hill is Starkfield's favorite sledding ground. Surely you are meant to take note of it because it is mentioned three times in this opening description of the town. Straddling the Varnum's front walk are two black Norway spruce trees, and just across the street is the church, toward which Ethan is headed.

As he strides ahead, a thought flashes through his head—something about the quality of the atmosphere on this cold, starry night: "It's like being in an exhausted receiver," he thinks. Such a notion in the mind of a scientist would be odd enough, but in Ethan's head it seems downright peculiar. Then you discover something about Ethan's past that explains why he might harbor such an idea.

NOTE: In *Ethan Frome* Wharton ignores the usual concept of time used in most fiction. She leaves it to the reader to figure out what comes first, second, third, and so forth. In an instant she takes you back years into the past, returns you to the present, then tells about events that may have occurred a week ago. Then just as suddenly she focuses on last winter. For example, the action in this opening chapter of Ethan's story takes only seconds to complete. But in the few moments it takes him to reach the church and peer in the window, we catch glimpses of events that took place last year as well as half a dozen years ago.

Ethan had attended a technological college in Worcester, but because his father was killed he dropped out after a year. Ever since, images of what he had learned come to him unexpectedly. You are told that Ethan has a fanciful mind that seeks deep meanings in ordinary events. It's an apt description. Notice his thoughts as he looks through the church window and observes the dancing inside.

Evidently Ethan doesn't want to be seen outside the church. He avoids the rays of light shining on the snow and hugs the shadows until he finds the window he wants. It seems clear that he's done this before.

NOTE: The contrast between the brilliant light inside the church and the darkness outside is drawn vividly. It couldn't be accidental. Look for the motif of light and darkness throughout the novel. Why does Wharton stress it? Could it be that darkness suggests secrecy? You already know that Ethan is, if nothing else, a secretive sort of fellow. Yet he reveals many of his most personal thoughts while at the church window

Inside the building it looks like the end of a cheerful, noisy evening of music and dancing. Suddenly a young man rounds up the crowd for the last dance, a lively Virginia reel. In the darkness Ethan's heart is beating fast, as though he himself is one of the dancers. However, his pulse quickens not from the dance but from the anticipation of finding in the throng a particular girl with a cherry-red scarf on her head.

He spies her dancing with Denis Eady. She's obviously enjoying herself. In fact, she's having too good a time to suit Ethan, who studies her closely and tries to interpret her every smile and movement. That she finds pleasure dancing with that no-good Romeo, Denis Eady, bothers Ethan greatly.

Clearly love has seized Ethan's heart, but it's not a joyful love. Rather, it's more of a plague. Why else would he be lurking in the shadows feeling jealous?

A moment later you learn the reason for Ethan's pain: He's already married to someone else. The story of how he got himself into such a dilemma starts to unfold.

The girl is Mattie Silver, a cousin of Ethan's wife, Zeena. For the past twelve months Mattie, who is about twenty-one years old, has been living with the Fromes, earning her keep by doing housework and aiding Zeena, who is in poor health. You will discover later in the story why Mattie came to Starkfield from Stamford, Connecticut, where she grew up. All you know for the moment is that hardship drove her to her cousin's house about a year ago.

The moment Mattie stepped from the train Ethan fell for her. To him she was "like the lighting of a fire on a cold hearth." She brought laughter and the exuberance of youth into the house. Most of all, she enabled Ethan to show off his knowledge of natural phenomena. He pointed out the constellations and lectured her on rock formations. Ethan and Mattie drew closer to each other because they both delighted in sunsets, clouds, and the sights they saw together in the fields and woods.

In contrast, throughout their marriage Ethan and Zeena have hardly talked to each other. Zeena spends most of her time alone, tending to her ailments. When she speaks it's usually to complain or scold. She is dissatisfied with Mattie's work around the house and grumbles about the girl's inefficiency.

Actually, Zeena has a point, for Mattie lacks the aptitude for housekeeping. Now and then Ethan neglects his own work in order to help Mattie with hers. One day Zeena discovered Ethan churning butter (Mattie's task) and turned away in silence after giving him "one of her queer looks."

Did that look indicate that Zeena knows his private thoughts about Mattie? Ethan thinks she does. On the other hand, perhaps he's just feeling guilty and imagines hidden barbs in Zeena's actions and words. He recalls one conversation in particular. One dark morning as he dressed and shaved, Zeena informed him that she'd spoken to her doctor, who told her never to be without help in the house. What will she do, she asks Ethan, after Mattie leaves. They can't afford to hire another girl.

"Why on earth should Mattie go?"asks Ethan.

"Well, when she gets married, I mean."

Ethan, noticeably flustered by Zeena's talk about Mattie's departure, can't continue to discuss it. "I haven't got the time now; I'm late as it is," he says.

She replies sharply, "I guess you're always late, now that you shave every morning."

That comment frightens Ethan more than any other because it is a fact that he started shaving daily only since Mattie moved into the house. He thought mistakenly that Zeena didn't notice such things about him.

Does Zeena know his private thoughts? He suspects that she does. But if he thought it over rationally, he'd probably realize that he needn't fret over his suspicion, for Zeena is caught up in her own woes and lacks the vision to see beyond them. But because Ethan doesn't judge others very astutely, he can't help worrying about what Zeena knows. Nevertheless, his worries won't drive Mattie from his mind. He broods about her virtually all the time.

And that's exactly what he's doing as he stands outside the church window on this chilly winter evening. He has come to escort Mattie home, and he's excited by the prospect. The two-mile walks that he and Mattie have been taking from the village to the farm have become precious to him. Those night walks have brought him and Mattie together. With her arm in his, they have gazed at the stars and reveled in the beauty of nature.

The passion he has for Mattie, however, is tarnished by feelings of uncertainty. Although she acts as though she's fond of Ethan, she appears to act the same way with Denis Eady as they dance together on the other side of the window. Every time she smiles at Denis, Ethan grows less sure of himself. He berates himself and wonders how his dull talk could ever interest her.

NOTE: In just a few seconds Ethan's state of mind has fluctuated from extreme happiness to terrible despair, then back again. His mood swings occur throughout the book, often very rapidly. The dark and light images you saw earlier in this chapter reflect the state of Ethan's emotions. Because he has dark thoughts much of the time, dark images, black shadows, grays, and other muted colors dominate the book. You'll see them time and again.

The dance is about to end. Ethan stands there confused and unhappy. Self-doubt, Zeena's threats, and Mattie's ambiguous hints of affection cloud his brain as the chapter closes.

NOTE: Wharton's personal diary reveals that she wrote *Ethan Frome* during a time when she was in love with an American newspaperman stationed in Paris. The affair troubled her greatly, not in a moral sense, but rather because the man's interest in her was sometimes physical, sometimes intellectual, but never both. In short, he kept her off balance. Knowing this, you can hardly overlook the parallels between her experience and Ethan's.

CHAPTER II

Poor Ethan! Without a shred of self-confidence he stays hidden in the shadows as the dancers pour out of the hall. Instead of coming forward, offering Mattie his arm and heading toward home, he waits behind the door to see what Mattie will do. Ethan hasn't felt this shy in a long time. Mattie's easy manner has rubbed off on him a little bit, but tonight he feels "heavy and loutish" again.

Outside the church Mattie looks around expectantly, but still Ethan hangs back. A man approaches her. It's Denis Eady. He offers to take Mattie home in his father's sled. She needs a little coaxing, so Denis jokes with her, telling her that he "kinder knew" she'd want to take a ride tonight. He brings out the sled and turns back the bearskin blanket to make room for Mattie at his side.

NOTE: Ethan is repulsed by Denis' flirtatious manner. In fact, he has always been disgusted by "cheap banter." You will see that in college he was nicknamed "Old Stiff," presumably because he couldn't loosen up. Repeatedly in the novel Ethan will be unable to say what's on his mind. His inarticulateness causes him pain, as you might expect. It's also one aspect of an important theme—isolation. Being unable to express himself sets him apart from others.

Watching the scene, Ethan waits in agony, as though his life depended on what Mattie decides. Will she get in, or won't she? Mattie declines Denis' invitation and starts to walk away. Denis thinks she's just playing hard to get and urges her to climb aboard, but again she says no. Denis jumps from the sled and takes her arm, but she eludes him. Finally, he gives up and drives away.

Ethan scurries after Mattie and catches up with her in the black shade of the Varnum spruces. She is glad to see him, but he is almost bursting with joy that she turned Denis away. Also, he's impressed at how clever he's been to spy on her. Now he wants to dazzle Mattie with a memorable turn of phrase, but the best he can do is, "Come along."

Isn't it sad that Ethan, hoping for a rush of eloquence, can think only of "Come along"? How difficult it is for him to break out of his shell.

Before starting home they pause at the top of the steep hill on the Corbury road, where sledders have left numerous tracks. Ethan and Mattie decide to sled here tomorrow night if there's a moon. She tells him news of Ned Hale and Ruth Varnum— soon to be Mr. and Mrs. Hale. While coasting here, they almost ran into the big elm at the bottom of the hill.

NOTE: The description of Corbury hill may be of interest because it shows you a section of Starkfield. But later the site will assume much greater importance in the story. By having Ethan and Mattie notice the tracks and the elm tree, the author is preparing you for a return visit much later in the novel. You might not notice Wharton's use of foreshadowing the first time you read the book. When you are well along in the story, however, think back to these early chapters. You won't find many details in this carefully designed work that are included by chance.

The thought of Ned and Ruth being killed is especially chilling because, as Mattie declares, "They're so happy!" To Ethan, Mattie's words sound as if she had been thinking of herself and him.

NOTE: You've just been introduced to a pattern in Ethan's behavior that you will encounter again and again. Ethan has momentary illusions often, but not always, relating to Mattie. Why he suffers from spells of self-delusion is not altogether clear, but it's not uncommon for a person who is unhappy with reality to escape to a fantasy world once in a while. We all do it, but perhaps not as frequently as Ethan.

Ethan relishes the moment, but his joy is short-lived. A few seconds later Mattie speaks to him indifferently, and his spirits sink. The slightest change in Mattie's look and tone can buoy Ethan's mood or send him into despair. Tonight he tends toward desperation. He needs some assurance that Mattie cares for him. As they walk he tries to draw out her feelings: "I suppose . . . you should be leaving us." She thinks Zeena plans to send her away, but she tells Ethan indignantly that she won't go unless "*you* want me to go too—"

Unless *he* wanted her to go! Her response thrills him. As far as he's concerned, Mattie will stay with him forever. Again he gropes for words that will express his feelings. Again he can't find them, and settles for a feeble "Come along."

Nearing the house Mattie and Ethan pass through the Frome family graveyard. For years the sight of the headstones has reminded Ethan that like his ancestors he was doomed to live and die right here on his Starkfield farm. On this night his urge to flee the farm has vanished. He thinks that staying here with Mattie is all he'd ever want, and when they die, they'll lie together in this cemetery.

What can be said about a man who dreams of dying during his brightest moments? Certainly he's a morbid fellow. But beyond that, Ethan knows that happiness with Mattie is just not meant to be. He can't face the fact, however, so he deludes himself with a dream that can't come true.

When Mattie stumbles, he steadies her and slips his arm around her. She doesn't resist. What bliss! Triumphantly they walk across the frozen snow "as if they were floating on a summer stream."

Suddenly the thought of Zeena intrudes. In his mind's eye Ethan sees Zeena "lying in their bedroom asleep, her mouth slighty open, her false teeth in a tumbler by the bed. . . ." What a letdown! From bliss to bitterness in an instant. Ethan notices a dead cucumber vine on the porch, dangling like a black streamer tied to a door to signify a death. He wishes such a streamer had been hung there for Zeena.

Standing outside the door, Ethan tries one more time to tell Mattie what he feels. "Matt—" he says. And that's all. The rest of the words remain unsaid.

NOTE: "A granite outcropping." What did Ethan want to say? You could probably finish his sentence without difficulty. Most people can say something like "I love you" to someone they adore. But Ethan, for the time being at least, doesn't know

how. His passion is trapped inside. Have too many
years with Zeena and too many winters in Starkfield encased him permanently in a rock-hard shell?
Further along in the story you're bound to find
out.

Wharton, in describing her intention to create a
"New England" character, calls Ethan a "granite
outcropping." There is a great deal of granite in
the New England states, but more to the point is
that granite is a hard, sturdy rock that doesn't break
or erode easily.

Ethan thinks that as usual Zeena has probably
been in bed since just after supper. The door key
will be under the mat. But Ethan can't find it. A
wild thought tears through him: Some tramps have
been seen in the neighborhood. What if they. . . .
He never finishes the thought, but you can finish
it for him. Remember that cucumber vine on the
front porch? Ethan has thoughts of death—and
maybe even murder—constantly in his mind, although nothing you've seen so far ought to suggest he could kill another person—except perhaps
in one of his illusions.

Ethan hears movement inside the house. Again
he thinks of the tramps, but it's Zeena who has
come down to open the door. Now you catch your
first glimpse of Zeena in the flesh. Until now
you've only heard about her. Edith Wharton intends us to see Zeena as particularly ugly—sort of
an old crone. Ethan notices, as though for the first
time, her "flat breast," her "puckered throat," and
the deep "hollows and prominences of her high-
boned face." What a contrast to Mattie who has

"the colour of the cherry scarf in her fresh lips and cheeks."

NOTE: You're seeing here one of Wharton's favorite stylistic techniques—the use of parallel descriptions. First she presents the unsightly Zeena in all her ugliness. In striking contrast she shows Mattie a line or two later. Keep this scene in mind. You'll see a parallel scene later in the story, but instead of Zeena, Mattie will be standing in the kitchen door.

Entering the house is like going into "the deadly chill of a vault." Why wasn't Zeena in bed? To explain, she says, "I just felt so mean [sick] I couldn't sleep." Is she telling the truth? Or has she stayed up to haunt him and Mattie, as Ethan suspects? Although there's no way to tell just yet, what's your guess?

Zeena lives up to her reputation as a crank: She turns a cold shoulder to Mattie and scolds Ethan for tracking snow into the house. Then she walks out of the kitchen expecting them to follow her up the stairs to the bedrooms.

Ethan hesitates. He doesn't want Mattie to see him following Zeena to bed, especially on this night of nights. He offers a lame excuse for staying downstairs in the cold, unheated kitchen. Mattie flashes Ethan a look which he interprets as a warning. Perhaps Mattie, too, thinks that Zeena has become suspicious of them. To play it safe, Ethan ascends the stairs behind his wife and disappears into the bedroom.

Have you noticed that since Ethan's story began, no more than two hours have passed?

CHAPTER III

Early the next morning you find Ethan and Jotham Powell, the hired man, in the woods cutting and hauling lumber. Ethan plans to sell the lumber to Andrew Hale, the Starkfield builder. He likes being out in the fresh morning air, where he can do his clearest thinking.

Ethan's thoughts turn back to last night. He and Zeena had gone silently to bed. For a while he had lain awake listening to Mattie moving about her room across the hall. He had stared at the crack of Mattie's light shining under his door. Doesn't Ethan seem like a teenager in love? He's so infatuated with Mattie that he wouldn't sleep until she turned off her lamp.

NOTE: While Ethan lies in the darkness with Zeena by his side, his eyes are glued to Mattie's light. You've seen the dark-light motif before, but never so clearly. Images of light—sun, fire, Silver (Mattie's last name) materialize almost every time Ethan looks at Mattie. Note, too, that light is akin to warmth. Whenever Mattie appears, the temperature rises, and you may find a reference to summer. Similarly, Zeena brings on the darkness and creates a chill wherever she goes.

Then all was silent except for Zeena's asthmatic

breathing. What keeps coming back to him now is the memory of Mattie's warm shoulder pressed against his. He regrets his failure to kiss her when he had the chance.

How Mattie has changed since she came to Starkfield! So thin and pale at first, so fresh-faced and pretty now. Ethan recalls how Mattie had shivered during the first cold winter. But she had never complained. According to Zeena, Mattie had to make the best of it because she had no place else to go. (You can always depend on Zeena to strike a low blow. If she has a sympathetic streak in her, Edith Wharton keeps it well hidden.) In any case, family misfortune had, in effect, bound Mattie to them, much like an indentured servant.

Mattie's fate, it seems, was determined by her late father's recklessness with money. Orin Silver, Zeena's cousin, left the Connecticut hills for Stamford, where he married and took over his father-in-law's "drug" business. (Notice that Wharton puts *drug* in quotes, suggesting that Orin's business was slightly shady.) Orin had ambitious plans. From his wife's relatives he borrowed large amounts of money, which he promptly spent or lost. He died young. When his wife found out the real nature of the business, she died too, leaving Mattie a pauper.

NOTE: Money—or its absence—shapes the lives of the characters, determining what they can and cannot do. Many important decisions are based on money, and it is a major theme in the novel. In addition, Ethan worries about it constantly. While he suffers from a shortage of money, his story is rich with allusions to it. Note also that Mr. Silver's first name means "gold."

To earn a living Mattie tried stenography and sales, but her health broke. Her relatives declined to help. They took out their anger with Orin on his poor daughter, giving her nothing but advice.

When the doctor advised Zeena to look for household help, Mattie fit the bill. What Zeena liked especially was that she could scold and find fault with the girl to her heart's content. Mattie had to take it; she couldn't quit.

On the surface the Frome household appears peaceful. As a stranger, you probably wouldn't notice Ethan's tension. And you surely would not observe his vague dread about the future. But what happened last night—especially Mattie's sudden look of warning in the kitchen—has alarmed him. It has triggered a feeling that something quite awful, perhaps a blow-up between Zeena and Mattie, will soon take place.

Ethan trudges home from the sawmill, to be on hand if a fight starts. To his surprise, he finds Zeena wearing her best dress and bonnet, with a suitcase packed. Her pain is so severe that she's going to consult a new doctor in Bettsbridge, where she'll spend the night with her Aunt Martha Pierce.

Ethan's reaction is a little surprising. Wouldn't you expect him to feel ecstatic? Zeena will be gone for a day or so, and he'll be left alone in the house with Mattie. Instead, his reaction is relief. He's relieved to know that last night Zeena had spoken the truth. She was in pain, and she had not stayed up to harass Mattie and him, after all.

Even though Ethan can breathe easier now, he's not altogether happy, for he's worried about the cost of Zeena's trip. Two or three times she has traveled to see a doctor, each time bringing home expensive but useless remedies and health devices.

But Ethan's worry is promptly chased from his mind by one overwhelming realization: Mattie and he will have a night alone in the house. He wonders if the same thought has occurred to Mattie.

Before you look in on Mattie and Ethan spending a night together, Zeena must be taken to the train. She expects Ethan to drive her, but he can't wait to be rid of her. He arranges for Jotham Powell, the hired hand, to take her. His excuse is that he intends to collect cash for the lumber delivery he'll make to Mr. Hale that afternoon.

As soon as Ethan speaks these words he regrets them. Not only is he lying, but he knows that Hale won't pay cash. He never has. Moreover, to let Zeena think that he has money on hand is a terrible mistake, for now she's bound to go on a spending spree in Bettsbridge.

NOTE: Here's an instance of still another problem with words that plagues Ethan. As you've seen, words sometimes fail him. At other times, he says things that he regrets later. Ethan seems too stiff to blurt words out without thinking, but he does so. Moreover, he possesses an impulsive streak that leads him repeatedly into trouble. Notice the irony of his predicament: He can't find words which will help him but he is able to phrase those words which will get him into a fix.

CHAPTER IV

If you've ever entertained a terribly irritating guest for a long time, you can appreciate Ethan and Mattie's relief after Zeena drives off. Suddenly they can relax. Mattie hums in the kitchen, and Ethan prepares to haul lumber to town. He'd like to stay near Mattie, of course, but he also wants to be home before nightfall. After a casual "So long, Matt," he is off.

All the way to Starkfield he envisions their evening together: He'll smoke his pipe; they'll talk and laugh while sitting by the stove like a married couple.

Ethan's spirits soar in anticipation. How odd to see this ordinarily silent and somber man whistling and singing. It's been years since his mood has been this cheerful.

Ethan can be affable, but he's had few chances recently to show it. Ever since college he's led a solitary, more or less silent, life. After his father's fatal accident Ethan carried alone the burdens of the farm and mill. He had no time to linger in town with other young men. Then his mother fell ill. Although she could talk, she rarely did, so Ethan lived in a silent house. In fact, "the loneliness of the house grew more oppressive than that of the fields." And the long silent winters didn't help, either.

NOTE: The quiet of country life appeals to many people. But the kind of profound silence that Ethan has endured tends to be excruciating. It's more than mere absence of sound, for it connotes loneliness and isolation. You can't break the silence even if you try, for no one will hear you. The heavy snow of winter intensifies the hush and keeps people apart.

In Ethan you find a human counterpart of the silence and isolation of a Starkfield winter.

Ethan's imprisonment in a silent world ended when Zenobia Pierce, a cousin, came from the next valley to help care for his mother during the last stages of the old woman's illness. If you can imagine it, Zeena's voice was "music in his ears." Not only that, Zeena took charge of the sickbed and household duties. At once, Ethan was set free. He started tending the mill and farm full-time again.

Out of gratitude and the fear of being left alone on the farm after his mother's funeral, he asked Zeena to stay and marry him, which she did. They made plans to sell the farm and mill as soon as they found a buyer, for Ethan was eager to live in a large town, where he might work as an engineer. Zeena also wanted to leave their isolated farm.

But no one would buy their place. And, as Ethan discovered to his dismay, Zeena needed to be noticed. She couldn't tolerate being one of the crowd in a large town. What was worse, however, was that a year into the marriage Zeena took sick. Her "sickliness," observed Ethan, gave her just what she wanted—a reputation in the community. Zeena became a famous sick person.

Sickness silenced her, but maybe Ethan was partly at fault, too. Zeena didn't say much because, as she claimed, Ethan "never listened." But who can blame him? Zeena spoke only to complain.

Zeena's silence troubled Ethan just the same. Could she have turned into one of those sad, deranged women known to inhabit certain lonely farmhouses in the area? He wondered whether Zeena kept still to conceal suspicions about Mattie and him.

Except for one gnawing thought, his mind is at ease as he rides to town. He regrets telling Zeena he'd get cash for the lumber. No doubt she'd nag him to pay for a new patent medicine or a wonder drug for her ailments. But far more important, the money might renew her interest in hiring a girl to replace Mattie.

Andrew Hale and his wife were longtime acquaintances of Ethan's family. Zeena occasionally called on Mrs. Hale, who in her youth had cared for many sick people. For Zeena, visiting Mrs. Hale was next best to seeing a doctor. Hale himself ran a fairly prosperous construction business, but the demands of a large family kept him from becoming wealthy. Indeed, he was always a little "behind" in paying his bills. In the past he'd waited three months before paying Ethan for the lumber he bought. Obviously, it won't be easy for Ethan to pry the cash from Hale for this delivery, and he knows it.

After Ethan unloads the logs he sits down in Hale's office. Embarrassed, he asks Hale for an advance of fifty dollars. As expected, Hale says no, he can't pay. He treats Ethan's request almost humorously. In fact, Hale says, he had hoped for a little extra time to pay this debt because business is off slightly, and he's fixing up a little house for Ned and Ruth, who will soon be wed. Ethan could cite his own need for prompt payment, but he's too proud to plead poverty. He leaves the office empty-handed.

While attending to other business in Starkfield,

Ethan hears the jingle of sleigh bells. It's Denis
Eady, who dashes by with a hearty greeting for
him before heading his sleigh out of town, maybe
toward the Frome farm. Ethan suspects the worst.
He thinks that Denis, hearing that Zeena has gone
to Bettsbridge, plans to visit Mattie for an hour or
so. Jealousy storms in Ethan's heart, just as it did
last night.

Before he leaves Starkfield he is stung by jealousy again. As darkness falls Ethan passes the
Varnum spruces. In the shadows he sees and hears
Ned Hale and Ruth Varnum kissing. The two young
lovers separate when they realize they've been
spotted. Ethan finds momentary pleasure in having interrupted Ned and Ruth at the very place he
and Mattie had stood less than twenty-four hours
before. But he realizes enviously that Ned and Ruth
don't have to hide their happiness.

NOTE: As Ethan goes about he utters hardly a
word to anyone, yet through his thoughts you become better acquainted with him. Edith Wharton
favored revealing her thoughts by means of long,
inner soliloquies. Her friend, Henry James, en-
couraged her to use dialogue sparingly and to write
it only when the conversation would bring out sig-
nificant and distinctive qualities of the speaker. The
reason: people are usually honest in their thoughts.
In conversation with others, you can never be sure.

With spirits ebbed again, Ethan starts home. He
listens for Eady's sleigh bells, but the lonely road
is silent. Near the farm he notices the light in Mattie's room and he guesses that she's dressing for

supper. He recalls how on the evening of her arrival, Mattie appeared for supper with smoothed
hair and a ribbon at her neck, and how Zeena stared
at the girl sarcastically.

As always, Ethan passes his family graveyard.
He glances briefly at the headstone of an ancestor
also named Ethan Frome, buried with his wife,
Endurance. The inscription says that the pair had
lived together "in peace" for fifty years. Bitterly,
Ethan wonders if he and Zeena would have the
same epitaph.

In the barn, Ethan is relieved to see that Denis
Eady's horse is not there. Perhaps he didn't come
this way, after all.

The kitchen door is locked, just as it had been
the night before. He calls out to Mattie, who comes
to open the door in a minute or two. Ethan (and
perhaps you, too) is struck with how similar tonight's homecoming is to last night's. Instead of
facing Zeena's witchlike countenance, however, he
is greeted by Mattie's shining face. Last night the
kitchen had seemed like a chilly vault; tonight it's
warm and friendly. The table is set and a bright
fire is lit. Ethan is almost overcome with a sense
of well-being.

Unable to contain himself, Ethan wants to know
for sure if Denis Eady had paid a call on Mattie.
"Any visitors?"

"Yes, one," answers Mattie. A blackness settles
on Ethan, but it vanishes instantly when Mattie
says the visitor had been Jotham Powell. Since
Jotham had driven Zeena to the train, Ethan asks
instinctively if she got there on time. Immediately
he regrets mentioning Zeena's name, for it throws
a chill between him and Mattie.

All through supper they feel Zeena's presence

in the room. The cat jumps between them into Zeena's empty chair. (You're not told whether it's a black cat, but it probably ought to be.) Zeena's name keeps coming up in their conversation; it's almost as though she has cast a spell over them. Ethan has things to say to Mattie. He wants to be eloquent. At the mention of Zeena, however, he becomes inarticulate and talks about the weather.

This evening was meant for celebration. Why can't they enjoy a pleasant supper together? Are they so guilt-ridden by illicit thoughts?

NOTE: Guilt has long been associated with the New England personality. It probably originated in Puritan days, when rules about how to conduct your daily life were very strict. If you broke the rules you were punished severely, but physical punishment wasn't enough. In fact, the pain inflicted on you served to cleanse your wrongdoing. If you could be made to feel guilty, too, then you suffered more and were less apt to break the rules again.

From Zeena's chair the cat jumps onto the table and heads toward the milk-jug. Ethan and Mattie reach for the jug at the same time. Their hands meet and clasp for a moment longer than necessary. Unnoticed, the cat backs off and knocks the pickle-dish onto the floor. The dish shatters.

"Oh, Ethan, Ethan—it's all to pieces. What will Zeena say?" Mattie cries out.

Ethan says to blame the cat, but Mattie knows Zeena won't be satisfied. Zeena had kept the dish safely on the top shelf of the china closet for the past seven years. It had been a wedding gift, so special that it was not meant to be used. (In a sense the dish was like Zeena herself—tucked away uselessly in the dark.) The dish can't be replaced, either.

When Mattie begins to cry, you realize how strongly she fears Zeena. But Ethan comes to the rescue, taking the fragments of the dish and reassembling them on the shelf. From below you can't tell the dish is broken. Months might pass before Zeena discovers the break. In the meantime Ethan will check nearby towns for a duplicate dish.

What confidence Ethan shows here! For a few moments forlorn Frome gives way to firm Frome. It's a side of his personality you haven't seen before. And what inspires his burst of self-assurance? A weeping Mattie and an opportunity to outwit Zeena. Or perhaps it's panic: He's so intimidated by Zeena that he'll do anything to avoid her wrath. Regardless, his performance impresses Mattie. She calms down, and he feels proud of how he handled the crisis of the pickle-dish.

CHAPTER V

Supper is over. You'll now see whether Ethan's dream will be realized—whether he'll have a cozy evening by the fire with Mattie.

Mattie sits by the lamp with a bit of sewing. Feeling content after a good day's work, Ethan stretches his stocking feet to the fire and lights his pipe. He asks Mattie to sit closer, for he wants to look at her. When she settles in Zeena's rocker, Ethan has a momentary shock. He sees Zeena's face instead of Mattie's.

NOTE: This domestic scene is never as blissful as it seems. You saw at supper how Mattie and Ethan feel Zeena's presence in the house. She haunts this scene, too. Symbolized by the cat, Zeena has a firm hold on Ethan's conscience. Her grip will tighten as the book goes on.

Uneasy in Zeena's place, Mattie moves back by the lamp. The cat, like a stand-in for its mistress, jumps into the vacant chair and through narrowed eyes watches Mattie and Ethan converse.

They talk naturally and simply of everyday things: the weather, Starkfield gossip, the next church social. Eavesdropping on them, you'd think this is just another evening in a long string of evenings they have shared. Ethan knows they're pretending to be married, and he'd like to continue the illusion as long as he can.

At length he says to Mattie, "This is the night we were to have gone coasting." His tone suggests that they'll go another time. "We might go tomorrow if there's a moon." Seeing Mattie's enthusiasm, he becomes bolder. He describes the perils of coasting down the Corbury road, especially at the corner down by the big elm. "If a fellow didn't keep his eyes open he'd go plumb into it," he says. Neither Mattie or Ethan wants to be frightened half to death on Corbury road, so they agree that maybe they're better off staying home.

NOTE: You heard them talk of the menacing elm tree earlier in the story. Why should this big tree demand so much attention? Later you can count on the presence of the elm tree to touch the lives of the principal characters.

Mention of the Corbury road emboldens Ethan to reveal what he'd been thinking about all evening. He says to Mattie that under the Varnum spruces "I saw a friend of yours getting kissed." Ethan hopes that talking about Ruth and Ned's kiss might somehow lead to some small intimacy between him and Mattie. But as soon as he has spoken the words, he wishes that he hadn't, for they were too vulgar and out of place. And they make Mattie blush to the roots of her hair.

NOTE: Why might Mattie turn crimson so quickly? In the era when the story takes place, etiquette forbade talk in mixed company of virtually every bodily part and function. To talk of kissing or more intimate matters in the presence of unmarried girls was especially improper. Like any social practice, the custom was probably ignored as often as it was honored. But Mattie is either too scared or too naive to break the rules.

Mattie's embarrassment forces Ethan to keep his distance. He alludes to Ruth and Ned's impending marriage, a thinly disguised effort to talk to Mattie about her future. Does she want to marry? He could ask her directly, but he won't dare. "It'll be your turn next," he suggests. Slightly annoyed and a bit nervously, Mattie wonders whether Ethan has

raised the topic again because Zeena has something against her. "Last night she seemed to have,"
she explains. Again, Zeena intrudes.

To talk openly of Zeena's attitude toward Mattie
has suddenly moved Ethan and Mattie's relationship to a new stage. They've never spoken as can-
didly to each other as they do now. Feeling like
conspirators who have gone too far, they agree to
stop talking about Zeena. They understand each
other with perfect clarity, it seems, a rare moment
of two minds in perfect harmony. Ethan slides his
hand cautiously toward Mattie, and his fingertips
touch the end of the fabric she is sewing. The tension between them is electric.

All of a sudden, a sound! The cat jumps after a
mouse, sending Zeena's empty rocker into a ghostly
movement. Ethan is struck with a painful thought
that Zeena herself will be rocking there at this time
tomorrow, and he'll never have another dreamlike
evening such as this. His body and brain ache with
his sudden return to reality. A terrible weariness
takes hold of him. He doesn't know what to do or
say. Unaware of what he's doing, he stoops his
head and kisses the bit of cloth in his hand. Mattie
has already begun to roll up her work, and the
cloth glides slowly from his lips.

So ends Mattie and Ethan's evening together.
They arrange the room for the night, say good night,
and go upstairs separately. When Mattie closes her
bedroom door Ethan remembers "that he had not
even touched her hand."

CHAPTER VI

Consider the high hopes Ethan had for his evening with Mattie. Wouldn't you expect him to be

sullen with disappointment the next morning? But at breakfast he's irrationally happy. Why? Nothing in his life has changed. He had not even touched Mattie's fingertip. His cheerfulness mystifies even him.

He reasons that last night he had tasted life with Mattie, and he'd done nothing to spoil it. He feels good about that.

NOTE: Ethan feels proud to have resisted temptation. He could have thrown himself at Mattie. Had she resisted—which is very likely—the evening would have been spoiled. Moreover, she might have told Zeena about his advances, or she might have packed her bags and run away. In short, Ethan felt he had nothing to gain from giving in to his impulses. Therefore, he kept a cool head. Bravo, Ethan!

Later, setting off to work, he's tempted to tell Mattie, "We shall never be alone again like this." Again he resists, aware that a deeper involvement with Mattie can go nowhere. Instead he says matter-of-factly, "I guess I can make out to be home for dinner." (By "dinner" Ethan means the midday meal.)

He has a tight schedule for the day's chores: He must haul lumber to the village, buy glue, and repair the pickle-dish before Zeena returns. If all goes well he'll complete his tasks and still have time left to spend alone with Mattie. But all does not go well. A sleet storm has coated the roads with ice. The logs are slippery and take twice as long to load onto the sledge. One of his horses slips and falls, injuring a knee which Ethan must wash and bind.

Because of the delays Ethan postpones his trip to Starkfield until after dinner. He must hurry to be back before Zeena arrives. In the village he works frantically to unload the logs, then hastens to Michael Eady's shop for the glue. Ethan finds Denis Eady lounging with friends around the stove. Denis, clerking for the day, doesn't know where the glue is kept. Impatiently Ethan waits for Denis to search the shop. To Ethan, who's in a dreadful hurry, Denis seems to dawdle deliberately. The search is in vain.

NOTE: Have you noticed that each time Denis Eady shows up, Ethan feels as though he's been slapped in the face? Denis is probably a fine fellow, but to Ethan he is a threat, for Denis is a legitimate suitor for Mattie's hand. Furthermore, Denis' heartiness and cheerful personality make Ethan squirm. He can't return Denis' warm greeting or a slap on the back.

Ethan rushes to Mrs. Homan's shop, where the widow Homan hunts down her last bottle of glue, asking Ethan questions about his need for it and talking all the while. Glue in hand, Ethan dashes out and quickly mounts his sled. The widow calls after him, "I hope Zeena ain't broken anything she sets store [values] by." Mrs. Homan's words are lost on Ethan, but not on you. You might almost guess that Ethan's purchase won't remain a pri-

vate matter very long, and that somehow Zeena is
bound to find out.

Ethan drives home as quickly as he can, again
thinking of what Mattie might be doing. There's
no sign of Jotham, who's been sent to pick up Zeena
at the train. As Ethan enters the house, he shows
Mattie the glue and heads straight for the pickle-
dish in the china closet. She grabs him by the sleeve
and whispers, ''Zeena's come.'' They stand and
stare at each other like culprits caught in the act.
Has their plan been foiled? Not if Ethan can help
it. He assures Mattie that he'll come down to mend
the dish that night.

''How is she?'' Ethan wants to know. He's curious about Zeena because after her trips away from
home, she usually comes back ''nervous.'' That is,
she's even more snappish than usual. Mattie can't
tell because Zeena said nothing when she came in.
She hurried straight to her room.

In the meantime Jothan returns. Ethan invites
him to supper, thinking Jotham will serve to keep
things calm at the table. He turns down the invitation. Since Jothan won't walk away from a free
meal very often, Ethan senses that there's a mes-
sage in his refusal. Is it that Zeena didn't see the
doctor? Did she dislike his advice? Or is it some
other news? Ethan feels apprehensive about the
approaching meal, even though Mattie has prepared the room and table as attractively as on the
previous night.

CHAPTER VII

Ethan goes cautiously to greet his wife.
Zeena sits in the darkened bedroom, bolt up-

right, still wearing her traveling clothes. Something is wrong. Ethan's effort to be friendly falls flat.

"I'm a great deal sicker than you think," she announces, an edge of pride in her voice. The words sound ominous, but not to Ethan, for Zeena has cried "wolf" too often. She and her husband have held this conversation before. This time, however, Ethan thinks: what if at last Zeena's words are true?

You know immediately what Ethan is thinking. He may long for Zeena's death, but he says kindly, "I hope that's not so, Zeena."

"I've got complications," says Zeena, which means that she is not just sick, but *seriously* sick. In fact, she just might die. Ethan is suddenly tossed between waves of jubilation and pity for Zeena. She wants his sympathy, but she looks so hard and lonely sitting in the darkness that the best Ethan can do is question the reliability of her new doctor.

"Everybody in Bettsbridge knows about Dr. Buck," says Zeena. She cites the case of Eliza Spears, a woman Dr. Buck brought back from near death.

NOTE: You're not told what's wrong with Zeena, but she and her doctor think it's grave enough to require surgery. Medical practices in Ethan's day were still fairly primitive, and operations were often performed only as a last resort. Besides, people shunned operations, regarding them as "indelicate." Zeena, of course, disdains operations. After all, what violates your privacy more than a surgeon's knife? Ethan can be grateful, for he saves a great deal of money in surgeons' fees.

More or less convinced—or perhaps only resigned to Zeena's trust in Dr. Buck—Ethan asks
what treatment the doctor prescribes. Notice that
he is more curious about the treatment, which will
cost him money, than about the diagnosis.

"He wants I should have a hired girl," says Zeena,
and "I oughtn't to have to do a single thing around
the house."

What news could hit Ethan harder? Any treatment would be cheaper than hiring a full-time, live-
in housegirl. Still worse is that the matter has already been settled. Zeena's Aunt Martha has found
a girl who will arrive in Starkfield by train late
tomorrow afternoon.

Anger and dismay seize Ethan. He doubts that
Zeena is as ill as she claims, and is convinced that
she had gone to Bettsbridge as part of a scheme to
force a servant on him.

Enraged, he asks, "Did Dr. Buck tell you how I
was to pay her wages?" Just as furiously, Zeena
shouts back, "No, he didn't. For I'd 'a' been
ashamed to tell *him* that you grudged me the money
to get back my health, when I lost it nursing your
own mother!"

The two fling biting criticism and charges at each
other "like serpents shooting venom." This is the
first time open anger has raged between them in
seven years of marriage. When their wrath is spent,
Ethan feels ashamed over stooping to such sense-
less savagery. Moreover, lashing out at Zeena won't
solve the practical problem of having a new girl on
his hands the next day. "I haven't got the money
. . . You'll have to send her back," he tells Zeena.
He even vows to do everything around the house
himself. Zeena scoffs at that and asks about the

fifty dollars Ethan collected from Andrew Hale for the lumber.

Yesterday Ethan was right. He should not have lied about Hale's cash payment, and again regrets words he has spoken impulsively. He stammers that the whole thing was a misunderstanding. He doesn't have the money, and won't get it for at least three months.

How will they work out their differences? Ethan pledges to work that much harder to please her and Mattie. Zeena's solution stuns him: she plans to send Mattie away.

At the look on Ethan's face Zeena laughs out loud. (He can't remember ever hearing her laugh before.) Ethan has misunderstood. She never intended to keep two girls in the house. No wonder he worried over the expense.

Zeena's laugh is so wicked, you can't avoid the sensation that it signals her triumph over Ethan. She has successfully dealt him a blow below the belt.

Ethan can't believe it. "Mattie Silver's not a hired girl. She's your relation," he says. But Zeena regards Mattie as a pauper who's outstayed her welcome, and "it's somebody else's turn now."

No sooner has Zeena finished condemning Mattie when the young girl's cheerful voice calls them to supper. When Zeena refuses to go down, Mattie gaily offers to bring food up.

NOTE: You can't ignore the contrast between Zeena's coldheartedness and Mattie's innocent goodwill in this and several following scenes. Your sympathies lie with Mattie, of course. Yet bear in mind that Zeena is the wronged partner in the marriage. After all, it's not she who becomes involved, however innocently, in an extramarital relationship.

Ethan sweeps to Mattie's defense. "You ain't going to do it, Zeena?" But Zeena holds firm. Then follows one of the longest speeches Ethan makes in the book. Although it's only four sentences, it's spoken with great passion and intensity. It's clear to Zeena that Ethan is frantic to hold on to Mattie. "If you do a thing like that what do you suppose folks'll say of you?" he asks her. She shoots back a cutting reply: "I know well enough what they say of my having kep' her here as long as I have."

NOTE: Zeena's answer implies that village people have been talking about Ethan and Mattie, although you won't find evidence of such gossip in the book. Also, where could Zeena have heard such talk? She rarely sees anyone from Starkfield. Then what does she mean? Was her comment just a lucky stab in the dark? Don't you wish that Ethan would call her bluff and say, "Now what is *that* supposed to mean?" But Ethan is scared, and couldn't bear to have his relationship with Mattie exposed.

Ethan scowls at Zeena. This evil, brooding woman has robbed him of a happy life. Now she intends to deprive him of the one thing that could make up for every hardship he has suffered. Violence wells up inside him. He takes a wild step toward her and clenches his fist. But suddenly the flame of hatred goes out, and like a lamb he goes downstairs to tell Mattie the news.

Mattie serves Ethan his dinner, but he can't eat. He rises from his chair and walks around the table to her side. She looks at him, frightened. In terror she melts against him. "What is it—what is it?" she stammers. In answer, he presses his lips against hers. For an instant she's swept away by the intensity of his passion. Then she backs off.

Ethan says, "You can't go, Matt! I'll never let you go!"

"Go—go?" she stammers. "Must I go?"

Ethan breaks the news to Mattie, who droops before him "like a broken branch."

NOTE: You might wonder why Ethan doesn't put his foot down and declare himself boss. A coup d'état would spare himself and Mattie a good deal of heartache. Does he have the strength to defy Zeena? He's yet to stand up to her. Is he likely to start now? In addition, because Zeena is kin to Mattie and Ethan isn't, Zeena technically has the right to determine Mattie's fate.

Ethan knows that when Zeena makes up her mind, that's it! Mattie *must* go. But where? She has no home, no family, no prospects for work. She's hopeless in the truest sense of the word. Ethan despairs to think of her facing the world alone. He's reminded of tales of unfortunate girls seeking work in big cities and, in the process, losing their decency.

Ethan springs up suddenly. "You can't go, Matt!

I won't let you! She always had her way, but I mean to have mine now—" He stops in mid-sentence, hearing Zeena's footsteps behind him—and says not another word. So much for Ethan's rebellion.

Zeena takes her place at the table. Grim-faced as always, but unusually chipper, she heaps food on her plate, adjusts her dentures, and digs in. Her conquest of Ethan must have improved her appetite. She has a scrap of meat and an affectionate word for the cat. (A reward for being a faithful stand-in, perhaps?) Matter-of-factly she answers Mattie's questions about her visit to Bettsbridge. She cheers up—and even smiles a little—when describing the "intestinal disturbances among her friends and relatives." She addresses her cousin as "Matt," something she rarely did. What she says to "Matt," however, is that the pie she served for dinner "sets a mite heavy" in her stomach. In other words, it gives her indigestion.

Zeena has some rarely used heartburn medicine stored somewhere, and presently leaves the table to fetch it. In a few moments, she returns, "her lips twitching with anger, a flush of excitement on her sallow face." In her hands she carries the pieces of the red glass pickle-dish.

"I'd like to know who done this," she says, visibly upset. In fact, she's more distraught than angry. Tears hang on her eyelids. Her voice quavers as she explains how she put her precious pickle-dish on the top shelf of the closet to keep it safe.

NOTE: Zeena is obviously shaken by the discovery of her broken pickle-dish. But what causes such distress? Doesn't she seem to overreact? The dish has sentimental value because it came from her Aunt Philura in Philadelphia. But does Zeena seem like the sentimental type? Perhaps she is terribly hurt by Ethan and Mattie's deception. All we know for sure is that Zeena's response to the breaking of her treasure is way out of proportion to its monetary worth. For a moment she seems like a poor pathetic soul, perhaps deserving a little pity.

Ethan responds, "The cat done it," which is true to a point. But Zeena scoffs. Mattie then speaks out and accepts the blame.

"*You* got down my pickle-dish—what for?" Zeena wants to know. When Mattie explains, Zeena thunders, "You wanted to make the supper-table pretty, and you waited till my back was turned. . . . You're a bad girl, Mattie Silver, and I always known it."

If Zeena had any doubts or pangs of conscience about letting Mattie go, she's free of them now. She feels perfectly justified in casting Mattie out to her fate.

To cap her outburst Zeena leaves the room carrying the pickle-dish as if it were a dead body. She thinks aloud that this tragedy would not have occurred if she had listened to folks and sent Mattie away long ago.

CHAPTER VIII

That night, after Zeena falls asleep, Ethan comes downstairs to a small room which he sometimes uses as a study. He has some thinking to do.

As he lies down on the sofa-bed, a hard object

jabs his cheek. It's a needlework cushion, the only one Zeena ever made. Cushions are usually soft, but not this one. Remember, it's Zeena's. Ethan flings it across the room, and props his head against the wall instead.

What to do about Mattie weighs on his mind. Earlier in the evening she had left a note on the kitchen table. "Don't trouble, Ethan," it read—the first words she had ever written to him. How dismaying that in the future he would reach Mattie only with dead words on cold paper.

But Ethan does want to "trouble" about Mattie. He can't let his hopes die. He's only twenty-eight. Why should he give his life to Zeena? She's a hundred times meaner and more discontented now than when he married her.

Ethan thinks about a man much like himself who had lived over the mountain. The man escaped from his miserable wife by going West with the girl he loved. There followed a divorce, a remarriage, even a baby girl. The abandoned wife had sold the farm and opened a thriving lunchroom in Bettsbridge.

The story fires Ethan's thoughts. He'll do the same—leave with Mattie, take her West, and try his luck. He begins to compose a good-bye letter to Zeena, which she'll find on the bed after he's gone. "Zeena, I've done all I could for you," he writes. ". . . Maybe both of us will do better separate . . . you can sell the farm and mill, and keep the money—"

NOTE: You probably know Ethan well enough to speculate on why he decides to write a letter to

Zeena instead of telling her and walking out. Would she call him ludicrous and laugh in his face? Is he a coward? Is this another of Ethan's self-delusions? Or is he simply avoiding another vicious argument?

The word *money* gives him pause. What money will he use to carry out his plan? The farm and mill are mortgaged to the limit. No one would lend him a dime. In the West he'd surely find work, but it costs money to go West. Alone he would take a chance, but with Mattie in tow. . . ?

And Zeena? Ethan frets about her, even as he plans to run from her. She'd be lucky to earn a thousand dollars by selling the farm—if she could even find a buyer. When Ethan worked day and night, the farm provided only a meager living. Well, he thinks, she can leave the farm and try her luck with her family. See what they can do for her. Give her a taste of the bitter medicine she was trying to force on Mattie.

Ethan's eye falls on an advertisement in an old newspaper in the room. The ad announces "Trips to the West: Reduced Rates." Eagerly he reads the list of fares, and in a moment realizes the truth. There's no need worrying about how to live in the West because he doesn't have the fare for the trip. There is no way out—none. He is a prisoner for life, and he knows it. Lying back on the sofa-bed he weeps and gradually falls asleep.

Waking at dawn, he feels chilly and stiff. He's jolted by the thought that Mattie leaves today. What he'll do without her, he can't imagine. Suddenly Mattie enters the small study and tells Ethan that she had lain awake all night listening for him to come upstairs.

Although this is her last morning, she starts the day like any other, doing her chores. With the daily routine begun, Ethan thinks he may have exaggerated Zeena's threats last night. He's hopeful that in the light of a new day, she may come to her senses. But he must wait until Zeena awakens to know if his hunch is right.

Outside, Ethan sees Jotham Powell arriving for work as usual. All is so ordinary, Ethan can't believe that this will be an exceptionally sad day in his life. Jotham, however, reports that Dan'l Byrne will be taking Mattie's trunk to the train at about noon. According to instructions from Zeena, Jotham plans to take Mattie to the station afterwards—in time to catch the six o'clock train to Stamford.

"Oh, it ain't so sure about Mattie's going—" suggests Ethan. But Jotham—and maybe Ethan himself—knows that Zeena clings to her decisions. When the two men go inside for breakfast, they find Zeena unusually alert and active, the way you'd expect a child to be on a special day. She announces the day's schedule, laying to rest any doubt that Mattie will leave today.

Now it's the eleventh hour for Ethan. He's got to do something, but what? One thing he's sure about, he's not going to sit around the house and look on helplessly as Mattie is banished.

He starts to town, being reminded as he walks of happy moments he shared with Mattie at this tree or that bend in the road. Suddenly it occurs to him that he still has one chance to raise funds for his trip West. Andrew Hale might pay his debt if he knew that Zeena's poor health required Ethan to hire a new servant. Pride wouldn't keep Ethan from asking Hale for payment this time. Just this once, Ethan thinks, he might resort to lying. His best tactic, he knew, would be to enlist the help of Mrs. Hale, a kindly person, who could be persuaded to help Ethan plead his case to her husband.

NOTE: This is the first time you see Ethan plotting something openly dishonest. Would you call him a dishonest man, however? Do you think that his affair of the heart is dishonest? You may find it worthwhile to ponder the state of Ethan's morality.

Near town he catches sight of Hale's sled, with Hale's youngest son in the driver's seat, his mother beside him. What good luck! Just the person Ethan wants to talk to.

Mrs. Hale greets Ethan cordially. Immediately you see why she's considered a kind person. Her face has "pink wrinkles twinkling with benevolence." No one else in the book resembles her even faintly.

Mrs. Hale has already heard about Zeena's trip to Bettsbridge to see the doctor. She wishes Zeena well, and adds, "I always tell Mr. Hale I don't know what she'd 'a' done if she hadn't 'a' had you to look after her; and I used to say the same thing 'bout your mother. You've had an awful mean time, Ethan Frome."

At that Mrs. Hale nods sympathetically and drives away. Ethan is left standing in the middle of the road, struck dumb with shame and astonishment. Never in his twenty-eight years has anyone spoken so kindly to him. No one has understood his plight so well. Until this moment, no one has admired him like Mrs. Hale.

Ethan is not only surprised, he's overcome with guilt. To think he was going to take advantage of the Hales' sympathy to obtain money! To think he was going to lie to the only people around who pitied him! A scoundrel might deceive his friends, but not Ethan.

Slowly Ethan returns to the farm. He has suddenly recognized who and what he is: a poor man with a sick wife, "whom his desertion would leave alone and destitute."

CHAPTER IX

Can you doubt that Mattie will leave before the day is out? Can you doubt that something drastic will happen in this, the climactic chapter of the book?

Ethan acknowledges that Zeena has won a victory. In defeat, he enters the kitchen to find his wife reading a book called "Kidney Troubles and Their Cure," an undeniable clue to her condition.

NOTE: Zeena shows signs of suffering from a kidney problem, most likely a kidney stone. It would certainly be appropriate for her to have a hard, gritty rock growing inside her. On the other hand, doesn't she deserve sympathy, too, because the pain caused by a kidney stone is reputed to be

excruciating? It can turn the gentlest soul into a
tiger.

·He goes upstairs to help Mattie with her trunk.
There is no answer when he calls outside the bedroom. Opening the door he finds out why. She
sits on her trunk, sobbing.

"Oh, don't—oh, *Matt*!" he says to comfort her.
Startled to see him there, she clings to him. He
puts his lips to her fragrant hair. At that moment
Zeena calls from downstairs to hurry up and bring
the trunk, for Dan'l Byrne won't wait much longer.

Ethan hoists the trunk onto his shoulders and
carries it down the stairs. Zeena, absorbed by her
book, doesn't even look up as he goes by. Mattie
helps him lift the bulky trunk onto the sleigh, which
drives off in haste.

Each minute pushes Mattie and Ethan another
step closer to the moment that neither can face. To
put off the time when he must say good-bye to
Mattie, Ethan decides that he—not Jotham Powell—will drive her to the Flats to catch her train.
After the noon meal Ethan declares his intention
to Zeena.

"I want you should stay here this afternoon,
Ethan," his wife says. "Jotham can drive Mattie
over." Zeena has plans for Ethan to repair the stove
for the new girl. Ethan is determined to do as he
wants, however. "If it was good enough for Mattie," he says, "I guess it's good enough for a hired
girl." His temper surging, Ethan storms out of the
house. He'd rather face Zeena's anger later than
give up his last precious hour or two with Mattie.
While hitching the horse to the sleigh he recalls that

the day he first met Mattie, just over a year ago, was soft and mild, just like this one.

When he re-enters the house the kitchen is deserted. He finds Mattie, dressed to go, looking around his small study where he had slept last night. Is this the last time he'll see her standing here? Ethan refuses to believe it, still clinging to a hope that this is all a mistake. He shudders at the thought of returning home alone only a few hours from now.

Zeena won't bid Mattie good-bye. She's gone to her room and left word not to disturb her. So it's final! Zeena has achieved her goal. As far as she's concerned, it's good riddance to Mattie. When she comes downstairs again she will find a new girl in Mattie's place.

Although it's early, Ethan says it's time to go. He plans to take a detour to Shadow Pond on his way to the Flats. He wants Mattie to see the place where they once had picnicked together. During a church outing last summer he had come upon her surrounded by a group of young admirers. When she saw him approach, she broke from the group and gave him a cup of coffee. Then they sat by the pond on a fallen tree. He found a locket she had lost. Each remembers the lovely summer afternoon as a time of supreme happiness.

The pond is frozen now, but still beautiful. Seeing the place again gives Ethan a fleeting illusion that he is a free man, and that he's wooing the girl he intends to marry. For a few moments they spill out their hearts to each other. He'd like to whisper sweet words into her ear, but can't. In spite of loving feelings, he's never learned how to express his love.

NOTE: How fitting that the place where Ethan and Mattie began their fleeting romance be named Shadow Pond. Like a shadow, their love cannot last.

Like all pleasant dreams, this one ends too. The sun sinks behind the hill, turning the landscape gray again. They must resume their journey to the train.

"What do you mean to do?" Ethan asks.

Mattie doesn't know. Work in a shop will damage her health again. Relatives won't take her in, even if she were willing to ask them.

"You know there's nothing I wouldn't do for you if I could," he says.

"I know there isn't," she says. To prove it, she pulls from her dress the good-bye letter that Ethan had begun to write to Zeena last night. Mattie had found it in Ethan's study.

He is at once astounded and overjoyed that she read the letter. Would she have gone West with him? "Tell me, Matt! Tell me!"

"I used to think of it sometimes, summer nights. . . ," she answers.

Ethan's heart reels with the thought that Mattie has loved him since last summer—since Shadow Pond.

At this point can anything good come from such news? Won't it make their parting all the more painful? Perhaps, but knowing the depth of Mattie's feelings helps Ethan declare his love openly. For once his tongue sings without restraint: "I want to put my hand out and touch you. I want to do

for you and care for you. I want to be there when
you're sick and when you're lonesome." Rather
than have her married to someone else, he adds,
"I'd a'most rather have you dead. . .!"

"Oh, I wish I was, I wish I was!" she sobs.

What he has said suddenly shames him. "Don't
let's talk that way," he whispers.

By the time the sleigh nears the edge of the village, daylight has surrendered to darkness. Ethan
and Mattie hear the shouts of children. Some village boys have just finished their coasting for the
day. Mattie reminds Ethan that he was to have
taken her down the hill last night.

At the crest of the steep hill on the Corbury road,
he asks, "How'd you like me to take you down
now?" Mattie hesitates. Is there time? Ethan prom-
ises her that there's all the time they want. He'll
do almost anything, it seems, to postpone the moment of parting.

Under the Varnum spruces they find a sled that
probably belongs to Ned Hale. They prepare to
coast, Mattie in front and Ethan steering. It's very
dark, but Ethan laughs away the danger. "I could
go down this coast with my eyes tied," he boasts.

Down they fly. Approaching the perilous elm
tree near the bend in the road, Mattie shrinks back
against Ethan for safety. "Don't be scared, Matt!"
he cries as they make the turn and speed down to
the bottom of the slope.

They start the long walk up. Ethan wants to know
if Mattie had been afraid of the elm tree. "I told
you I was never scared with you," she answers.

At the top of the hill they return the sled. Standing in the shadows of the Varnum spruces Mattie
asks, "Is this where Ned and Ruth kissed each

other?" She flings her arms around Ethan. Two nights ago he had seethed with envy of Ned and Ruth. Tonight others might envy him and Mattie. Breathlessly, they kiss.

"Good-bye—good-bye," she stammers.

"Oh, Matt," he cries, "I can't let you go."

They cling and sob like children. "What's the good of either of us going anywheres without the other now?" he says.

"Ethan! Ethan! I want you to take me down again!" she cries, her tearful cheek against his face. ". . . So 't we'll never come up any more." She wants Ethan to steer the sled right into the big elm so they'd "never have to leave each other any more."

Ethan can't believe her proposal. "You're crazy!" he says.

NOTE: You might agree with Ethan that Mattie's urge to destroy herself and take Ethan with her proves that she is "crazy." But that's part of the tragedy. In a classic tragedy the hero ends up dead. Usually the hero yearns for death as a release from the suffering of life. Is Ethan better off dead? Mattie thinks so. She begins to list all the things wrong with life. Ethan listens and is convinced.

Mattie uses flattery to persuade Ethan to take a suicide run with her. No one in the world, she says, has ever been as kind to her. Then she pleads with him, conjuring up an image of life in his house with a new hired girl. He envisions the house and thinks of Zeena, the intolerable woman he would see every night for years and years.

These are powerful arguments, too strong for Ethan to repel. They cling to each other. He finds her mouth again. In the distance the train whistle blows. "Come," Mattie whispers, tugging him toward the sled.

The slope below them is deserted. All of Starkfield is at supper. They mount the sled. Suddenly, he springs up. "I want to sit in front," he says.

Mattie protests. "How can you steer in front?"

"I don't have to. We'll follow the track."

NOTE: Ethan adds that he's going to sit in front because he wants to feel her holding him on the way down the slope. That's a fair reason. But you can't help wondering if that's the only reason. By sitting in front, wouldn't he receive the full force of the impact with the tree? Or does he want to make sure he dies because he can't live without her? Has his self-destructive urge become stronger than hers? Deep inside, does he perhaps want her to survive the suicide attempt?

On the sled Mattie clasps Ethan. He leans back, and their lips meet one last time. The descent starts. It seems to Ethan that they are flying. The big elm looms ahead. "We can fetch it; I know we can fetch it—" he says, determined to hit the tree trunk squarely.

All of a sudden he thinks of Zeena's twisted, ugly face. For an instant he's distracted, and the sled swerves slightly from its deadly course. But he rights it again and drives it into the black mass of the tree. . . .

The story pauses for a moment. Have Mattie and Ethan "fetched" it? Ethan survives, of course. In the prologue of the novel you've already seen him many years after the smash-up.

And Mattie? You discover her fate at the same time as Ethan. Lying dazed on his back, he sees a star through the branches of the elm. Is it Sirius? he wonders. Too tired to think, he closes his heavy lids to sleep. The silence is profound. Is this like the moment of death?

Ethan hears a little animal squeak under the snow. It sounds like a frightened field mouse in pain, pain so intense he feels it in his own body. The sound seems to come from something soft and springy under his outstretched hand. Slowly things come into focus. His hand is resting on Mattie's head; the cries of pain come from her lips.

Faintly she speaks his name.

"Oh, Matt, I thought we'd fetched it," he moans in grief and agony. But both, to their regret, have lived through the smash-up.

What becomes of them afterward you will find out in the epilogue—that is, in the untitled last chapter of the book.

NOTE: Death pacts between lovers who cannot bear to part occur in both life and literature. Greek mythology tell of Baucis and Philemon, whose wish to die at the same moment is granted by the gods. In Dante's *Inferno* the lovers Paolo and Francesca kill themselves, but death brings them no relief from suffering. They are doomed to spend eternity in the second circle of hell, their punishment for yielding to desires of the flesh. Then too, Romeo and Juliet inflict death upon themselves, although technically not as a result of a prearranged agreement. Regardless of the time or place, stories of lovers' suicides almost never fail to stir the emotions.

EPILOGUE

The epilogue begins precisely where the prologue ended, twenty-four years after Ethan and Mattie crashed into the elm tree.

Ethan and his overnight guest, the narrator of the story, step into the Frome farmhouse. Two women in the kitchen stop talking when they notice the stranger.

Even before he's introduced the narrator is struck by the room's shabby appearance. The meager furnishings are soiled and worn from use.

Now that Ethan has come home one of the women—a tall, bony, gray-haired figure—starts to prepare the evening meal. The other woman remains huddled in an armchair near the stove. She can't get up because her body is limp. She can move her head, but that's all. She has the bright witchlike stare of someone suffering from a disease of the spine.

NOTE: Although the narrator needs to be told who these women are, you don't. You've met them before and know them well: Mattie and Zeena.

However, you're probably not ready for the shocking change that has taken place since you last saw them.

When Ethan comments that the room feels cold, the small woman in the chair explains in a high, thin voice that the stove has just been refilled with wood. She adds that her companion had taken a long nap and had neglected the fire. "I thought I'd be frozen stiff," she complains.

Ignoring the accusation, the tall woman returns to the table with dinner—the cold leftovers of a mince pie. As she sets the battered pie dish down, Ethan introduces her: "This is my wife, Mis' Frome."

"And this," he says, turning toward the shriveled figure in the chair, "is Miss Mattie Silver. . . ."

NOTE: The gap between the "first acts of the tragedy," as Wharton put it, and the moment when you meet Zeena and Mattie a generation later, has provoked a good deal of literary commentary. Henry James called it "peculiar." In response, Wharton said the book had to be organized this way to achieve the dramatic impact she sought. If the book had been longer, she may have structured it differently. But Wharton deliberately turned Ethan's tale into a novelette rather than a full-length novel to create a stark effect in both the story and its telling.

Back in Starkfield the next day, Mrs. Hale and

old Mrs. Varnum can hardly believe that their young boarder, the narrator, had spent the night under Ethan Frome's roof. Mrs. Hale tells him, "You're the only stranger has set foot in that house for over twenty years."

The fact that he gained admittance to Ethan's house makes the narrator something of a celebrity to his landlady. Now she can trust him with more information about what happened to Ethan, Mattie, and Zeena after the smash-up. In fact, Mrs. Hale seems almost relieved to spill out the painful memories she's kept bottled inside her these many years. Her loosened tongue brings Ethan's story up to date.

After the collision with the elm tree Ethan was carried to the minister's house to recover. Mattie, much more seriously hurt, was brought up the hill to the Varnum house. Ruth (now Mrs. Hale) was with her when she awoke. Mattie, seeing her good friend at her bedside, broke down and told Ruth everything.

Word of the accident spread around town, of course. But only Ruth knew why Ethan and Mattie had been coasting that night when they should have been on their way to the Flats to meet Mattie's train.

What Zeena thought nobody knows. To this day she's said nothing. Zeena had hurried to Ethan's side after the smash-up. Later, when Mattie was well enough to be moved, Zeena took her back to the farm, too. The crippled girl has lived there ever since.

"It was a miracle," says Mrs. Hale. Before the accident Zeena had been so sick, she couldn't even care for herself. But when the call came "she seemed to be raised right up." For over twenty years now she's had strength enough to care for both Ethan and Mattie.

Not that it's been easy, adds Mrs. Hale. Quite the contrary, in fact. Suffering has turned Mattie sour, and Zeena has always been a crank. Sometimes the two women torment each other. To see Ethan's face when Mattie and Zeena do battle would break your heart, for he's the one who suffers most.

On pleasant summer days Mattie can be moved into the yard, and there's some relief in that. But in winter the three of them are shut up in one small kitchen. New England winters last a long time. Can you understand now why Ethan goes to the Starkfield post office each noontime to pick up mail that almost never comes? No wonder, too, that his shoulders are stooped and his face is grim. Do you recall that Ethan's gaunt figure makes him appear as though he's "dead and in hell?" In a way, he is. As Mrs. Hale intimates, she doesn't see "much difference between the Fromes up at the farm and the Fromes down in the graveyard; 'cept that down there they're all quiet, and the women have got to hold their tongues."

A STEP BEYOND

Tests and Answers

TESTS

Test 1

1. The narrator fails to learn the whole story _____
   of Ethan Frome from the people in Stark-
   field because
   A. details of Ethan's past have faded
      from the townspeople's memory
   B. they are embarrassed by Ethan's
      behavior
   C. they don't know the whole story

2. The main reason that Zeena decides to let _____
   Mattie go is that Mattie
   A. broke the glass pickle-dish
   B. is a sloppy housekeeper
   C. keeps Ethan from caring for the farm
      and mill

3. Harmon Gow calls Ethan one of the "smart _____
   ones" because Ethan
   A. seeks larger meanings under the
      surface of things
   B. went to college
   C. deals shrewdly with Mr. Hale

4. The major causes of Ethan's suffering are _____
   I. his marriage to Zeena
   II. his love for Mattie
   III. his poverty
       A. I and II only   B. I and III only
       C. I, II, and III

5. Ethan decides that he can't run off with _____
   Mattie after all because
   A. Zeena would never grant him a
      divorce
   B. he can't afford it
   C. his conscience tells him it would be
      wrong

6. Ethan spends a period of his life in almost _____
   total silence because
   A. Zeena is too preoccupied with her
      ailments
   B. he lives alone
   C. his mother is too sickly to speak

7. Symbolic meanings may be seen in _____
   I. the glass pickle dish
   II. the missing "L" of Ethan's farmhouse
   III. Ethan's boots in the hallway
       A. I and II only   B. I and III only
       C. I, II and III

8. Mrs. Hale's comment, "You've had an aw- _____
   ful mean time, Ethan Frome"
   A. convinces Ethan to abandon Zeena
   B. helps Ethan to make peace with
      Zeena
   C. startles Ethan because he never
      expected it

9. Ethan defies Zeena when he _____
   A. spends the night in his study
   B. drives Mattie to the train
   C. refuses to pay Zeena's doctor bills

10. Ethan asks Zeena to marry him principally _____
    because he
    A. can't face being left alone on the farm

   B. is grateful for her help
   C. feels sorry for her

11. How does money—or its absence—influence the life of Ethan Frome?

12. What role does the winter season play in the novel?

13. To what extent is Ethan responsible for his own fate?

14. Which character in the novel suffers the most?

15. Discuss the notion of reality vs. illusion in the novel.

Test 2

1. Ethan leads a sad life and comes to an un-   _____
   happy end largely due to
   A. his loyalty to his family
   B. his pessimism
   C. his unwillingness to take risks

2. When Mattie arrives in Starkfield she is   _____
   A. anxious to start her new job
   B. weak, timid, and sickly
   C. planning to stay only a short time

3. When Ethan tells Mattie to "Come along,"   _____
   he
   A. has just realized that he loves her
   B. can't think of anything better to say
   C. is showing his jealousy of Denis Eady

4. Mattie does not realize that Ethan loves her   _____
   because
   A. she thinks of him as a second father
   B. he has never told her
   C. he is married

5. Ethan feels it is necessary to lie to Zeena _____
   about
   A. who broke the glass pickle-dish
   B. collecting money from Mr. Hale
   C. where he goes each night with Mattie

6. Allusions to death and dying occur _____
   throughout the novel because
   I. winter is a lifeless season
   II. life for Ethan, Zeena, and Mattie is
   no better than death
   III. they add to the mood of the story
       A. I and II only   B. II and III only
       C. I, II, and III

7. What Ethan likes best about his evening _____
   with Mattie is
   A. pretending to be married to her
   B. being rid of Zeena for a short time
   C. the dinner she prepared

8. Ethan suspects that Zeena went to Betts- _____
   bridge
   I. as part of a scheme to get rid of
   Mattie
   II. to prove to him that she was very
   sick
   III. to lay a trap for Mattie and him
       A. I and II only   B. I and III only
       C. I, II, and III

9. Seeing Ruth and Ned kissing under the _____
   spruces
   A. heightens Ethan's ardor for Mattie

B. makes Ethan envious of their
   happiness
C. embarrasses Ethan

10. Ethan realizes that he will never leave _____
    Starkfield after
    A. he drops out of college
    B. he marries Zeena
    C. he can't find a buyer for his farm

11. How does sickness influence the life of Ethan Frome?

12. How does the setting help to develop the novel's
    themes?

13. What if the story had been told by Zeena instead of
    Ethan? Comment on how it might be different.

14. Is Ethan "smart," as Harmon Gow says?

15. Discuss death as a motif in the novel.

ANSWERS
Test 1
1. C   2. B   3. A   4. C   5. B   6. C
7. A   8. C   9. B   10. A

11. Considering how often money is mentioned in the
novel, it must be important in the life of the main character. But usually it's a lack of money that affects Ethan.

Before Ethan's father died, the old man, in his delir-
ium, gave away much of the family wealth. Therefore,
Ethan starts out with little money. And when he marries
Zeena, he remains poor because Zeena spends the little
he earns on doctors and patent medicines.

Mattie enters Ethan's life because her father bilked

money from his wife's relatives. When he died, his debts could not be paid. Cast out of her family, Mattie came penniless to Starkfield.

It's the absence of money, too, that prevents Ethan from escaping to the West with Mattie. On his way to ask Andrew Hale to pay for a load of lumber, Ethan meets Mrs. Hale. Her kindly manner causes Ethan to change his mind.

The final blow-up between Ethan and Zeena occurs over money. Zeena has hired a new girl to replace Mattie. Because Ethan can't afford both to pay the new girl and to feed Mattie, Mattie must go.

Clearly there's plenty of evidence in the book to prove that lack of money helps to determine Ethan's lot in life. Although Ethan needs help, he's too proud to ask for it. Hale doesn't pay his debt because he doesn't know how poverty-stricken Ethan is, and Ethan won't tell.

12. Ethan claims that he would not have married Zeena had his mother died in the spring or summer. Why?

Do you remember that Ethan feared being left alone on the farm in the dead of winter? Zeena remained his only hope of avoiding utter loneliness. Other events in the novel hinge on the fact that it is winter; for example, Ethan and Mattie's fateful sled ride and the snowstorm that trapped the narrator in Ethan's house. Review the story for other examples.

Setting the book in the wintertime also allows the author to create a certain mood. Winter is the lifeless season. In winter, people—especially country people—are often isolated inside their houses. The land is silent under a blanket of snow. Wharton could not have emphasized such themes as isolation and silence in her novel without the aid of the winter season.

Look at a winter landscape. What colors predominate?

Look through the book for white, gray, and black imagery. You should find an abundance of these colors.

13. This question invites three different responses: Ethan is totally responsible; he is not at all responsible; and he is partly responsible.

To use the first approach, think of all of Ethan's decisions. As a mature person he should be held responsible for marrying Zeena, for allowing her to dominate him, for allowing himself to fall in love with Mattie, and so forth. Since Ethan had the choice to do or not to do each of these, he must take the responsibility for his actions.

On the other hand you can think of Ethan as a victim of circumstances. After all, it wasn't his fault that Zeena turned out to be sickly. Also, can a man really prevent himself from falling in love? Moreover, Ethan didn't want to be poor; it just turned out that way. As for his personal qualities, can a man be blamed for being inarticulate or insecure, or being any other way?

To take the middle road, simply hold Ethan accountable for creating some of his problems, and let him off the hook for others.

14. This is a difficult question because you can make a case for any of the three main characters as the chief sufferer.

If you choose Ethan, emphasize how he suffers from loneliness and isolation. Show how he feels trapped—by Zeena, his poverty, his farm, and his personality. Being unable to speak the words on his mind gives him intense pain. His hopes for a better life are repeatedly destroyed. He suffers the anguish of loving a woman who, as far as he knows, does not return his love. And in the end, he lives out his years tormented by two women who constantly fight with each other.

Zeena suffers, too, although you're not likely to sympathize with her. Whether her illnesses are authentic or imagined, they are real enough to make her an invalid. To spend so much of one's life consulting doctors and taking medicine—all to no avail—takes its toll in suffering. In addition, no one can enjoy being trapped inside a repulsive body like Zeena's. Finally, she has a husband who would be unfaithful if he had the opportunity, and she spends two dozen years taking care of the woman who should be her enemy.

Mattie, too, has had a grim life, although she covers her suffering with smiles and a cheerful disposition—until the smash-up, at any rate. After that she is paralyzed from the neck down, totally dependent on others. Her suffering ages her long before her time. Of the three characters she certainly endures the most physical pain.

Read through the Themes section of this study guide for a discussion of reality and illusion. It provides examples of how Ethan is beset by dreams that never come true.

Beyond that you might consider the "reality" of the story. Could such a story really take place? Are the characters real or are they stereotypes? Or perhaps composites made up of different types?

Ask yourself these questions: Why does Ethan remain with Zeena? Why does Zeena come to the rescue in the end? Would two real people in Ethan and Mattie's circumstances agree to kill themselves? Would a man change his life plans after receiving an offhand compliment from the wife of a business acquaintance? Is life really as somber as Wharton presents it in her novel?

Remember, finally, that the story is told years after it happened. Did it happen the way the narrator tells it? Or is it safe to assume that the passage of years has distorted the story beyond recognition?

Test 2

1. A   **2.** B   **3.** B   **4.** B   **5.** B   **6.** C
7. A   **8.** A   **9.** B   **10.** C

11. The more broadly you interpret the word "sickness," the richer your answer will be. Obviously you can find many examples of physical sickness that touch Ethan's life. Zeena's illness traps Ethan on the farm, depletes his resources, and enables him to spend an evening alone with Mattie. Ethan would never have known Mattie at all if illnesses had not taken her parents' lives. At the same time he and Zeena became acquainted as a result of old Mrs. Frome's fatal ailments.

If you consider injury as a kind of sickness, you might also mention that Ethan abandoned his plan to become a scientist when his father lost his health from a kick in the head by a horse. Finally, the injury which Mattie suffered in the smash-up changes Ethan's life forever.

Just a list of sicknesses and injuries won't answer this question fully, however. What's the point of citing these examples? They prove that Ethan has been a victim of other people's maladies all his life. (See "The Tyranny of Sickness" in the Themes section of this study guide for a fuller discussion.) But they also create a mood in the novel. The characters are not only physically sick, they are also sick at heart. Their lives lack meaning; they suffer from dead souls. Although Ethan remains intact physically, he might as well be dead.

12. Before you answer, read the Themes section of this study guide. You'll find several references to Starkfield, especially Starkfield in the dead of winter.

Who would live in an isolated village but isolated people? The setting, therefore, contributes to each character's loneliness. For example, Ethan is out of touch not only with Zeena, but with his whole community as well.

Most of the novel takes place in the wintertime, the season of death. You see reminders of lifelessness in the barren land, the dormant trees, the town buried under snow. Ethan walks past his family graveyard going to and from work every day, keeping him ever mindful of his fate.

The snowbound countryside helps to develop the theme of silence. If you've ever been in a snow-covered, windless place far from civilization, you know the eerie sound of silence. In the novel the absence of sound extends into the lives of the characters. Ethan and Zeena rarely speak, and Ethan is tongue-tied much of the time. Moreover, for a long time he took care of his sick mother, who spent her last years almost mute.

Ethan and Zeena's story would be unlikely today. Many modern couples, as unhappy as Ethan and Zeena were, would probably split up. When Ethan and Zeena married, however, most couples remained united until they died. The theme of loyalty to one's marriage vows may now seem out-of-date, but not in a novel set in the years around 1900.

13. You can have some fun with this question. Would Zeena come down on Ethan as hard as he came down on her? Or would she be gentler? What would Zeena say about Mattie? Did she know about the relationship between Ethan and Mattie? Was Zeena as sick as she claimed? Would she present herself as a sympathetic figure? An abused wife? A good-hearted soul trying to save her marriage from the home-wrecker, Mattie?

You might also comment on specific scenes in the novel. For example, what did Zeena think when Mattie and Ethan came knocking on the kitchen door? What were her thoughts when she discovered the broken pickle-dish? Most fascinating of all, how did she come to terms with Mattie and Ethan's suicidal sled-ride? Why hadn't they gone directly to the train station?

On the night of the smash-up Zeena summons enough strength to abandon her sickbed forever. How she does so is never explained. How do you think she might explain it?

Changing the point of view in the novel opens up innumerable variations and possibilities. Let your imagination soar.

14. Because "smart" to Harmon may differ from "smart" to you, define the term. Since Harmon is an unlettered fellow, he looks up to Ethan for having gone to college and for being "aware of the huge cloudy meanings behind the daily face of things." That is, to Harmon, Ethan is practically an intellectual, a label that you may accept or reject.

If you take the term "smart" to mean knowledgeable, Ethan is smart in science, in farming, and in sawmill operations. He also knows how to care for horses. You can probably assume that he's well informed about other matters, too, but you won't find evidence in the book.

Factual information aside, is there anything that Ethan should know, but doesn't? Most likely, yes, because he would not have such a difficult time in life if he knew, for example, how to manage Zeena. Nor can he deal with other people very handily. You can probably think of many other instances when Ethan gets into trouble, bungles a job, or makes an error that a "smarter" person might have avoided.

By no means is Ethan dull; however, living where and as he does, he has few opportunities to show his intelligence. On the other hand you might think that living where and as he does testifies to a weakness of character.

15. This topic is rich with possibilities. You might think first of how death shapes events in the story. The parents of both Ethan and Mattie die. Review the plot to see how these deaths eventually bring Ethan, Zeena, and Mattie together.

The story is crowded with reminders of death, including the Frome family gravestones with their morbid messages. The winter drains the life out of plants, buries the houses in snow, and so on. (See the Themes section of this guide for more examples.)

As important as the deaths of people and plants are the symbolic deaths suffered by the characters. Zeena, at least, cannot be said to live a life fit for humans. Every day Ethan seems to die a thousand times as he battles with insecurity, embarrassment, and a tongue that fails him.

Finally, Mattie and Ethan try to kill themselves. Because they fail, they are doomed to a living death.

Term Paper Ideas and other Topics for Writing

Character Analyses

1. Is Ethan Frome a tragic hero?

2. Is any character in the story heroic?

3. Who is the novel's villain?

4. Who or what is responsible for the sad fate of Ethan Frome?

5. How would the book be different if Zeena told the story? If Mattie told the story?

6. Do the characters control their own destinies?

7. How important are the novel's minor characters?

8. Would today's feminist movement object to *Ethan Frome?*

9. To what degree is the setting of the novel also a character?

Motifs and Symbols
1. How does the concept of reality vs. illusion help to shape Ethan and Mattie's love?

2. Why is *Ethan Frome* set in the wintertime?

3. Why does death play such a large role in shaping the novel?

4. How does Wharton's choice of symbols affect the mood of the novel?

5. What relationships exist between symbols and themes in the novel? Between symbols and characters?

6. How does money, or lack of it, help to shape the story?

Language and Structure
1. How does the language reflect mood or theme in the novel?

2. Why did Wharton choose to tell the tale as a remembrance of things past?

3. What is gained or lost by using the prologue and epilogue as a "frame" for the main story?

4. How does the narrator function? Does he have a role

in the novel, or is he merely a transmitter of information?

5. What is the significance of the names of places and people in the novel?

6. When and how does Wharton use foreshadowing in the novel?

Meanings of *Ethan Frome*

1. Is Edith Wharton correct in calling the novel a tragedy?

2. Does irony play a part in the novel?

3. Does the novel present a totally pessimistic view of life?

4. What does the novel say about the institution of marriage?

5. Is *Ethan Frome* a moral book?

6. Does the novel accurately depict life in New England in the early 1900s?

Further Reading

CRITICAL WORKS

On Edith Wharton

Auchincloss, Louis. *Edith Wharton*. University of Minnesota Pamphlets on American Writers, No. 12. Minneapolis: University of Minnesota Press, 1961. A brief and informative literary biography.

Auchincloss, Louis. *Edith Wharton: A Woman in Her Time*. New York: Viking Press, 1971. A biography, abundantly illustrated with family photographs.

Coolidge, Olivia. *Edith Wharton: 1862–1937*. New York: Scribners, 1964. This biography focuses on Wharton's personal life and loves.

Kellogg, Grace. *The Two Lives of Edith Wharton*. New York: Appleton-Century, 1965. A popular presentation of Wharton's life and works.

Lewis, R.W.B. *Edith Wharton, A Biography*. New York: Harper and Row, 1975. The definitive biography of Wharton.

On Wharton's Novels and Stories

Howe, Irving. ed. *Edith Wharton: A Collection of Critical Essays*. Twentieth Century Views Series. Englewood Cliffs, NJ: Prentice-Hall, 1962. A collection of essays devoted exclusively to Wharton's works, it contains something to interest everybody.

Kazin, Alfred. *On Native Grounds: An Interpretation of Modern American Prose Literature*. New York: Reynal and Hitchcock, 1942, pp. 79–90. Kazin is kind to some writers, but not to Wharton.

Lawson, Richard H. *Edith Wharton*. New York: Frederick Ungar, 1977. Stresses the social values depicted in Wharton's works.

Nevius, Blake. *Edith Wharton: A Study of Her Fiction*. Berkeley: University of California Press, 1953. A highly regarded study of Wharton's work.

On *Ethan Frome*

Lawson, Richard H. "Ethan Frome," in *Edith Wharton*. New York: Frederick Ungar, 1977, pp. 67–75.

McDowell, Margaret B. "Three Novellas about the Poor," in *Edith Wharton*. Boston: Twayne Publishers, 1976, pp. 64–72.

Nevius, Blake. "The Trapped Sensibility" and "The Remoter Imaginative Issues" in *Edith Wharton: A Study of Her Fiction*. Berkeley: University of California Press, 1953.

AUTHOR'S OTHER MAJOR WORKS

Italian Villas and Their Gardens, 1904
The House of Mirth, 1905
Madame de Treymes, 1907
The Fruit of the Tree, 1907
The Reef, 1912
The Custom of the Country, 1913
Summer, 1917
The Age of Innocence, 1920
The Glimpses of the Moon, 1922
A Son at the Front, 1923
The Writing of Fiction, 1925
Here and Beyond, 1926
Twilight Sleep, 1927
The Children, 1928
Certain People, 1930
The Gods Arrive, 1932
A Backward Glance, 1934
Ghosts, 1937
The Buccaneers, 1938

Glossary of People and Places

Andrew Hale   Starkfield's builder. Ethan delivers a load of lumber to him the day Zeena goes to Bettsbridge. Andrew is Ned Hale's father.

Aunt Martha Pierce   Zeena's aunt in Bettsbridge. Zeena spends the night at her house.

Aunt Philura Maple   Zeena's aunt from Philadelphia. The red glass pickle-dish was her wedding gift to Zeena and Ethan.

Bettsbridge   A town some thirty miles from Starkfield, where Zeena goes to consult a new doctor.

Corbury Flats   The closest railroad stop to Starkfield.

Corbury Junction   The site of the powerhouse where the book's narrator, a young engineer, works.

Corbury Road   The road to the Flats. In Starkfield the road has a very steep hill, down which Ethan and Mattie take their final sleigh ride.

Daniel Byrne   The sleigh driver who takes Mattie's trunk to the station.

Denis Eady   A young man in Starkfield whom Ethan considers a rival for Mattie's affection. Eventually he becomes a rich grocer and the owner of the local livery stable.

Doctor Buck   Zeena's physician in Bettsbridge. Because of his diagnosis of her ailments, Zeena hires a new girl to replace Mattie.

Ethan Frome   The main character. The novel tells of Ethan's life from his days as a young man until his early fifties.

Harmon Gow   Starkfield's stage driver in pre-trolley days, he is one of the narrator's informants about Ethan Frome.

Jotham Powell   The Fromes' hired man.

Lawyer Varnum   The town lawyer, he owns the Varnum house and is the father of Ruth Varnum, who marries Ned Hale.

Mattie Silver   Zeena Frome's cousin who comes to stay with Ethan and Zeena. She and Ethan fall in love, which leads to the story's tragic ending.

Michael Eady   Starkfield's Irish grocer, he's a clever businessman and also the father of Denis Eady.

Mrs. Andrew Hale   Mother of Ned Hale, she speaks sympathetically to Ethan, kindling such guilt in him that he cannot carry out his plan to go West with Mattie.

Mrs. Ned Hale   During part of the story she is Ruth Varnum, fiancée of Ned Hale. Later she is Ned's widow and owns the house where the narrator stays during his time in Starkfield. She was the first to see Ethan and Mattie after the smash-up.

Ned Hale   Son of Andrew and Mrs. Hale, he married Ruth Varnum.

Orin Silver   Mattie's father, whose death left Mattie destitute.

Ruth Varnum   Daughter of Lawyer Varnum, she marries Ned Hale. *See* **Mrs. Ned Hale.**

Shadd's Falls   Closest large town to Starkfield.

Stamford   Mattie's hometown in Connecticut.

Starkfield   Site of the story; its name suggests the kind of place it is—cold, desolate, and dreary.

Varnum   A well-known family in Starkfield. In front of the Varnum's house stand two large spruce trees that figure in the story.

Worcester   Site of the technical college that Ethan attended for one year.

Zeena Frome   Ethan's sickly wife, she is the odd person in the love triangle that blooms in the story.

The Critics

On the Authenticity of *Ethan Frome*

Because Edith Wharton came from a level of society so far removed from the poor country people who populate *Ethan Frome*, critics have regarded her so-called "New England folk tale" with considerable skepticism. A highly regarded scholar, Alfred Kazin, wrote:

> [*Ethan Frome*] was not a New England story and certainly not the granite "folk tale" of New England its admirers have claimed it to be. [Mrs. Wharton] knew little of the New England common world and perhaps cared even less. The world of the Frome tragedy is abstract. She never knew how the poor lived in Paris or London; she knew even less of how they lived in the New England villages where she spent an occasional summer.
>
> —*On Native Grounds: An Interpretation of Modern American Prose Literature*, 1942

Not all critics are as harsh as Kazin. Grace Kellogg, for example, agrees that *Ethan Frome* is not a New England story. In her opinion, the story was probably based on a French folktale, which Edith Wharton tried to transplant to Massachusetts. If the setting were the Alps,

> Ethan's character, which has been called too much of "granite" for the New England scene, orients itself at once on a bleak, isolated mountainside. Zeena's extraordinarily narrow, impervious nature finds a natural habitat there. As for Mattie, with her light gaiety, her innocence and purity and evanescent sweetness—she is the star-shaped blossom of edelweiss.
>
> The feeling of isolation which obtains, basic to the story despite all statements of country dance, village slide, friendly neighbors, a city not too far away, is now accounted for. . . .
>
> . . . That Starkfield "bobsled" has struck in many a critical craw. . . . [It's] a clumsy almost ludicrous vehicle, this New England bobsled, devoid of tragic

dignity. The toboggan of the folk tale offers no such
embarrassment.

—*The Two Lives of Edith Wharton*,
1965

On Style and Symbolism
Critic Blake Nevius writes with admiration of Edith
Wharton's use of vivid details:

> . . . they arise directly and easily, and always with
> the sharpest pertinence, from the significant grounds
> of character and situation. . . . Every reader will re-
> call some of them: Mattie's tribute to the winter sun-
> set—"It looks just as if it was painted"; Ethan's re-
> luctance to have Mattie see him follow Zeena into
> their bedroom; the removal of Mattie's trunk; the
> watchful, sinister presence of Zeena's cat disturbing
> the intimacy of the lovers' evening together by ap-
> propriating her mistress' place at the table, breaking
> the pickle-dish, and later setting Zeena's rocking
> chair in motion. Zeena may not be a sympathetic
> character, but there is a moment when she makes
> us forget everything but her wronged humanity. As
> she confronts the guilty lovers, holding fragments
> of her beloved pickle-dish, her face streaming with
> tears, we have a sudden and terrible glimpse of the
> starved emotional life that has made her what she
> is. The novelist's compassion can reach no further.
>
> —*Edith Wharton: A Study of Her
> Fiction*, 1953

The broken pickle-dish has attracted considerable critical comment. It has been viewed symbol-
ically in many different ways. This idea from Richard H. Lawson:

> The warmth of the evening is brought to an appre-
> hensive end by the accidental breaking of one of
> Zeena's sacred, never-used pickle-dishes. That the
> pickle-dish, a wedding gift, has never been used
> makes it a strong symbol of Zeena herself, who pre-

fers not to take part in life. The depth of Zeena's
reaction to its being broken is revealed by her an-
grily twitching lips and by "two small tears . . . on
her lashless lids."
                    —*Edith Wharton*, 1977

Critic Margaret B. McDowell considers the
pickle-dish an ironic symbol, closely related to other
ironies in the book:

Zeena is not seen simply as part of Ethan's curse
. . . but as a deprived woman who grieves over lost
beauty when the cherished red pickle-dish she has
saved since her wedding is used by Mattie and broken.
    The book is fraught with such ironies: the dish
that is treasured is the one that is broken; the pleasure of the one solitary meal that Ethan and Mattie
share ends in distress; the ecstacy of the coasting
ends in suffering; the moment of dramatic renun-
ciation when Ethan and Mattie choose suicide rather
than elopement ends not in glorious death but in
years of pain. The lovely Mattie Silver becomes an
ugly, querulous woman cared for by Zeena, who,
again ironically, finds strength and companionship
by caring for her former rival.
                    —*Edith Wharton*, 1976

NOTES

NOTES

NOTES